THE BAG
MAKING BIBLE

THE BAG
MAKING BIBLE

The complete creative guide to sewing your own bags

Lisa Lam   *Foreword by Amy Butler*

David and Charles
www.rucraft.co.uk

9359

Dedication

To a sweet and clever crafting friend if ever there
was one, my sister Jenny. My supportive and
encouraging family, Mum and Dad, Wendy
and Haymond. My craft widower husband, who
years ago prevented me from getting a 'real' job
and urged me to start up my own business.
Alan, thank you darling!

A DAVID & CHARLES BOOK
Copyright © David & Charles Limited 2010

David & Charles is an F+W Media Inc. company
4700 East Galbraith Road, Cincinnati, OH 45236

First published in the UK and US in 2010
Reprinted in 2010 (twice), 2011 (three times)

Text and designs copyright © Lisa Lam 2010

Lisa Lam has asserted her right to be identified as author of this work in accordance
with the Copyright, Designs and Patents Act, 1988.

A catalogue record for this book is available from the British Library.

ISBN-13: 978-0-7153-3624-3 paperback
ISBN-10: 0-7153-3624-X paperback

Printed in China by RR Donnelley
for David & Charles
Brunel House, Newton Abbot, Devon

Publisher Alison Myer
Acquisitions Editor Jennifer Fox-Proverbs
Editor James Brooks
Project Editor Ame Verso
Art Editor Charly Bailey
Photographer Jack Kirby and Lorna Yabsley
Production Controller Bev Richardson

David & Charles publish high-quality books on a wide range of subjects.
For more great book ideas visit: www.rucraft.co.uk

Contents

Foreword

Before I dig into the amazing details and inspirations behind Lisa's book I need to tell you a little bit about my dear friend Lisa. We met through email introductions when I learned that she was carrying my patterns and fabrics on her beautiful U-Handbag site. I fell in love with her blog and creative voice immediately and felt extremely honored to have such a passionate and talented partner. I sent her a speedy note with best wishes and received an overwhelmingly warm note in return. We quickly connected and found tons of things in common in both our working creative worlds and personal life. You know what it feels like when you've met a kindred spirit, an old soul who clearly is blessed with multiple gifts and incredible warmth? Well that's Lisa. I remember when I asked if she lived anywhere close to London and if we could meet in person. I had an upcoming book signing at Liberty's and she said 'sure, absolutely, no problem...' when in fact she had to travel fairly far and ended up spending the entire afternoon with me when she had oodles of bag orders waiting for her attention. That's just the kind of gal she is.

DAVID BUTLER

You get 150% of Lisa all the time. She's super smart and super talented and the best part is she makes herself available to everyone with her care, thoughtfulness wit and charm. She's pretty darn funny too, sly and always effervescent. Now she'd be the first person to scoff at my compliments, because she's very down to earth, but in this situation, I have the upper hand so she's just going to have to take all the praise! You need to understand these things about Lisa because that's how special this book is. True to form, Lisa gives so much of herself, her knowledge, experience, patience and limitless ideas for bag making... truly a bible indeed. She leaves nothing to chance because of her passion for empowering other sewists. She wants everyone to succeed and be inspired.

My favorite thing about this book is it is a storehouse of information that gives you all the tools to be completely creative and successful with your own bag inventions. Lisa sets up the chapters focusing on specific techniques with excellent behind the scenes information that give you the low down on tools and materials and follows that with great support visuals with her clear step by step how to photos. You'll find that Lisa's instructions are clear and visually very very easy to follow. The chapters conclude with inspiring images of stylish projects that apply the techniques first hand. So you get an amazing sewing education coupled with beautiful bags that of course, you can customize!

We're all so fortunate to get to know Lisa through her blog, web site and now her first book, which by all standards is one of the most comprehensive sewing books I've ever read. This will be one of your favorite go to books for ideas, inspiration and incredible how to reference. Lisa has given us all the tools to have a great sewing experience that will grow and grow. She's a special one!

I'm a very lucky gal to know her and am so happy to be able to tell you a little bit about Lisa and her wonderful bag making book!

Happy Happy Sewing!

Amy Butler

amybutlerdesign.com

Right *Lisa's beautiful Great Getaway Bag (see page 112) made up in home decor weight fabric from my Love collection. The fantastic design of the bag creates endless possibilities for use in your everyday life!*

Introduction

I love sewing. For me it is an indulgence, my work and a whole lot of fun. Inspired by my Mum, I've been sewing since I was a little girl. I have happy memories of the cool '70s flares and flowery pinafores that she used to sew for her groovy-looking kids. I've been unhealthily obsessed with fabric, haberdashery and sewing gadgets ever since. I'm self-taught, I love to experiment and I (usually) laugh at my mistakes.

Of all the things that I run up on my trusty sewing machine, bags are the thing that I enjoy making the most. Every girl needs a bag (or ten) in her wardrobe and a handmade bag is the perfect present to give at any time of the year. You can't beat the pleasure you get from owning a truly unique bag and the smug feeling you get from telling your amazed friends, 'Oh, I made it!'.

As this book will show you, you don't need to be a sewing whiz or to purchase exotic tools to make bags. You'll just need a sewing machine and some easy-to-obtain notions. While some of the bag projects in this book are aimed at the slightly more confident bag maker, you'll find that all of the bag-making techniques are suitable for all levels. So even if you are a beginner, this book will teach you how to add your choice of pockets, or insert a top edge zip to an existing bag pattern, for example. I have purposefully moved away from quick-and-easy bag projects because I believe that when you spend a little more time in creating something special you will cherish the results all the more. Fear not though, readers of my bag-making blog will know that I always try my best to write simple-to-follow instructions and to include plenty of helpful photos in all of my projects and techniques, and this book is no different.

Have you ever eyed-up other women's handbags and thought to yourself 'nice shape, but too few pockets' or 'too small' or 'yukky fabric' and so on? I thought so!

There's nothing wrong with wanting more pockets, a bigger bag, or even a fabric-matched purse for your glam party dress. But, as the saying goes, if you want a job doing well you have to do it yourself. This book will teach you how to do just that. It covers the basics from interfacings to pattern reading, and it contains eight scrummy bag projects. But best of all (for the first time in *any* bag making book) it also covers how to make the component parts of a bag, from different styles of pockets to making handles, from various bag closures to attaching linings, and much more.

Armed with the bag-making techniques inside this book, you'll be able to make the eight fabulous bags featured, but, crucially, you'll also be able to design and construct your own bags. Why be limited to mass-produced, shop-bought bags? Make your own bag your way and love it! If you fancy stepping up a level from homemade bags to handcrafted arm candy, step this way. All the techniques you'll need are right here …

Love bags; make bags!

Lisa

Visit me at my bag-making blog and say hello:
www.u-handbag.typepad.com

9

Basic Equipment

If you already enjoy sewing as a hobby, the chances are you already have most of the essential equipment for bag making. As with most things you get what you pay for, so buy the best you can afford and you'll need to replace items less often.

Cutting

- **Rotary cutter** – a rotary cutter greatly increases the speed and accuracy of fabric cutting. Also look out for rotary blade sharpeners, which will save you money on replacing dull blades.

- **Cutting mat** – for use with a rotary cutter. Choose one that has both imperial and metric gridlines (inches and centimetres). The gridlines are also really helpful when drafting your own bag patterns.

- **Dressmaking scissors** – choose scissors that cut all the way through to the tip, are as heavy as is comfortable (as the weight aids cutting stability), and are angled with the handles raised upwards.

- **Embroidery scissors** – small, fine-pointed scissors are essential for precision snipping.

- **Seam ripper** – not just for unpicking seams, a seam ripper is perfect for making tiny incisions for magnetic snaps and buttonholes. Always replace dull seam rippers to prevent you from having to push too hard, which could result in slipping.

Sharpen up ...
Keep blades on all cutting equipment sharp for safer and more precise cutting.

Marking, measuring and pinning

- **Disappearing marker** – this is my favourite type of marker because it is more precise than chalk. Make your marks as desired and they will disappear within 48 hours. Always do a test on a small swatch of your fabric to check first.

- **Hera marker (or bone folder)** – this useful marker makes an indent in your fabric from pressure only, so it is perfect if your fabric is unsuitable for a disappearing marker. It is also great for pre-creasing fabric when you need to make folds or pleats.

- **Tape measure** – to make measurement conversions easier, choose a tape measure with both metric and imperial measurements printed on the same side.

- **Sewing pins** – I love flower flathead pins because they are pretty and they prevent sore fingertips, sometimes caused by pushing pins through lots of layers.

- **Hand-sewing needle** – although you will be mostly sewing by machine, there are times when hand sewing is unavoidable – such as when the sewing machine can't reach the areas you need to stitch, or when sewing on buttons for example.

Bag-making tools

None of these tools are exotic or hard to obtain. They are all simple tools, which over the years I have collected. To make life easier and to get the best results from your bag making, try adding these items to your tool kit.

Thread For ease of use and to make long-lasting bags, use good quality all-purpose polyester thread. It might be tempting to buy cheaper thread but this breaks more easily, which makes it unsuitable for bag making.

Tape maker I use 2.5cm (1in) and 5cm (2in) tape makers to make bias tape for my own pretty piping and binding. See page 141.

Loop turner This simple tool is used for turning fabric tubes the right way out for speedy fabric strap making.

Bodkin A bodkin is used for speedy threading of cord or elastic through fabric tubes or casings. Attach the cord/elastic to the bodkin and thread the bodkin through your fabric tube.

Hammer and pliers Use a small hammer when you are working with rivets and eyelets (see page 85). Use two pairs of pliers for opening and closing metal rings and links in purse chains. Jewellery pliers are especially suited to those with small hands.

Fabric glue Use good-quality clear-drying fabric glue for when sewing isn't an option. Good fabric glue can be just as effective as stitching.

Tailors awl An awl is useful for making holes in fabric for rivets, poking out corners in fine straps (when turning out), or even coaxing small parts of your bag underneath the sewing machine foot (to help the feed dogs grab the fabric). Two types are available; one with a sharp point; the other with a ballpoint tip.

Mini bulldog clips Use these strong clips to hold pieces of fabric together temporarily when sewing pins are unsuitable, such as when your layers are very thick.

Hole punch Use a hole punch to cut neat holes in fabric for eyelets or popper snaps. This hole punch has various sized hole-cutter attachments and a smaller grip, which is great for small hands.

The Sewing Machine

A sewing machine is the most important tool in making bags (and sewing in general) but it doesn't need to be a grand or costly affair. There are only two features that I insist on: a powerful motor and a free arm (see below). The others listed here, while not essential, are useful to have. If buying a sewing machine and you want unbiased reviews and advice there are lots of good resources on the Internet. There are also numerous books available on getting the most of out of your machine, which are well worth investigating.

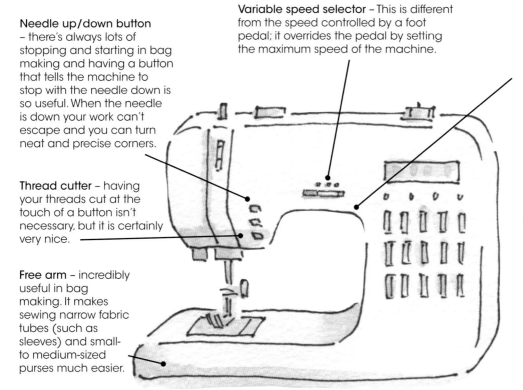

Needle up/down button – there's always lots of stopping and starting in bag making and having a button that tells the machine to stop with the needle down is so useful. When the needle is down your work can't escape and you can turn neat and precise corners.

Thread cutter – having your threads cut at the touch of a button isn't necessary, but it is certainly very nice.

Free arm – incredibly useful in bag making. It makes sewing narrow fabric tubes (such as sleeves) and small-to medium-sized purses much easier.

Variable speed selector – This is different from the speed controlled by a foot pedal; it overrides the pedal by setting the maximum speed of the machine.

Long arm – gives you extra table space to the right of the needle, great for when you are sewing large or bulky bags as there are times when you don't want to scrunch up your bag to fit it under the machine.

- **Powerful motor** – a must for coping with all of those fabric (and interfacing) layers.

- **Good stability** – when sewing at breakneck speeds or working with thick layers the last thing you want is your machine to shake and judder. Choose a machine that has a good weight and a wide stable base. Ask to see or test the machine in action at maximum speed.

- **Build quality** – how solid does the machine feel? I prefer heavy machines (the more metal the better) because they will last longer (with fewer machine services) and they will vibrate less.

- **Instruction manual** – I am a stickler for a good manual because no matter how experienced you are there will be plenty of occasions when you'll need to turn to

it for help. Don't be shy in the shop; ask to have a flick through the machine manual. Also look on the Internet for support and user manuals for your machine.

- **Bobbin winding system** – different sewing machines have different systems for bobbin winding. While in the shop, ask to see how the bobbin is wound and check you are happy with the method.

- **Dual feed system** – this is a feature on some machines that makes working with several and/or thick layers much easier because this system feeds the layers through the machine evenly and at the same speed. In normal sewing the bottom layer gets fed through the machine just before the top layer and this results in the top layer creeping forwards, which can be a real pain.

Machine feet

There are various feet required for different kinds of stitches and applications, so you need to think about the stitches you want to use and research to see which types of feet are appropriate for your needs. If you are about to purchase a sewing machine, see which feet are supplied with the machine, then ask the dealer if they will throw in some extra feet for free (and ask about any other freebies too!).

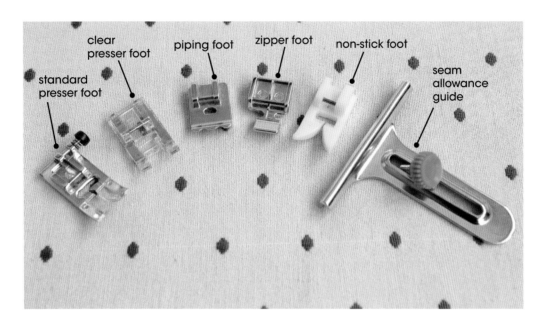

- **Standard presser foot** – this is the foot that you will make the most use of. With this versatile foot you can sew straight and zigzag stitch, and the majority of the more decorative stitches too.

- **Clear presser foot** – this is a standard presser foot, but instead of being metal, it's made from transparent plastic, which makes seeing things like notches and markings on your fabric so much easier.

- **Piping foot** – if you're going to sew with any amount of piping, a piping foot is a must, see page 145.

- **Zipper foot** – makes sewing very close to the edge of an item much easier, and is also essential for sewing zips.

- **Non-stick foot** – this foot is brilliant for 'sticky' fabric such as oilcloth, vinyl and leather (see page 32).

- **Seam allowance guide** – this is not a foot, but is a handy metal edge that screws to the bed of the machine and is very useful for professional-looking topstitching. Set your desired seam allowance on the guide, then butt the edge of your work to the seam allowance guide and away you go.

Machine stitches

I've been making bags for over six years and in that time I've only ever used two machine stitches.

Straight stitch This is basically the only stitch I ever really use.

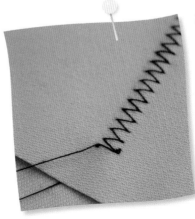

Zigzag stitch Every now and again I use zigzag to stitch over the raw edges of fabric to prevent it from fraying (see page 26).

Anatomy of a Bag

All bag designs vary in size, shape and purpose, but the bag part names are always the same, and the techniques used to create the various parts will be similar across different bag designs too. Bags can be as simple or as feature-packed as you want them to be. Have fun working through the techniques and projects in this book and you'll soon gain the confidence to design and make your own gorgeous arm-candy.

strap/handle

flap

strap attachment

closure

gusset

First impressions

- **Closure** – when it comes to closures there are so many options that there is a whole chapter of this book devoted to them – see pages 82–93. Your bag can be closed with several different types of zip insertions, a magnetic or invisible magnetic snap or a twist lock. A flap such as this one may also secure the bag closed, or be additional to a zip or snap closure. Mix and match closures for maximum versatility and functionality.

- **Gusset** – the design of the gusset often determines the capacity of your bag, as well as its silhouette. Gussets can be straight, have pleats or bellows, or even be adjustable using snaps or ties (see pages 52–53).

- **Strap/handle** – there are so many ways to carry your bag off in style that there is a whole chapter covering straps and handles – see pages 100–109. Choose handles that match the look and usability of your bag. Make your own or use convenient ready-made handles (see pages 110–111).

- **Strap attachment** – consider how the strap or handle is attached to your bag. There are numerous options, from stitching the strap directly onto the bag, to using fabric handle loops with metal rings (see pages 102–103), essential if making an adjustable sliding strap. Some straps can be attached permanently or others can be made with trigger hooks to allow them to be detached, either to transform the bag into a clutch, or to swap the handle for a different one to give a new look.

bag feet

bag back

bag bottom

Just around the corner

- **Bag bottom** – most bags beyond the simplest book bag will have some kind of bottom. Some will have a soft unstructured bottom, while others need a rigid, structured kind. If it's the latter, you may also want to add protective bag feet (see page 137). The right bottom can make all the difference to how a bag will sit on a surface and how it looks when full.

- **Bag back** – remember to give the back of your bag consideration too; if it's rubbing against your body as you carry it, then it needs to be streamlined and free of anything such as hardware or trimmings that will catch on your clothes or be damaged themselves. However it can also the perfect place for a secret, secure and easy-access slimline pocket, maybe flush and zippered (see pages 66–69).

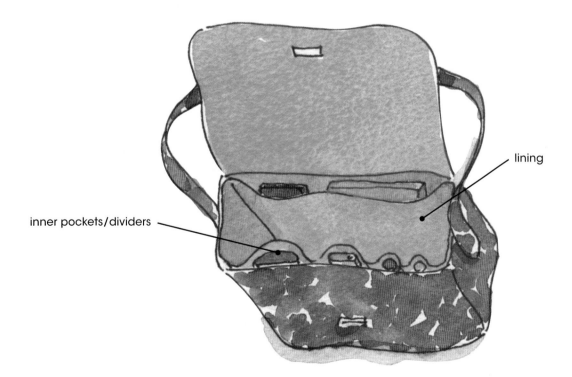

lining

inner pockets/dividers

What's inside counts

- **The inside of the bag** – this is equally important as the outside and needs to be given just as much care and attention. The lining is a chance to add lots of design features, from fabric choice (see pages 30–35) to the use of pockets and dividers for more organization (see pages 66–71). Joining the bag exterior to the lining is a fundamental part of the bag construction process, and there are two different methods to try, depending on the design of your bag (see pages 72–75).

1: GETTING STARTED

If you're anything like me you're probably keen to get stuck in with the scissors and sewing machine, and might be too impatient to read through this chapter. I totally understand, but even a quick read through the basics explained here could make all the difference between a bag that you will love and a bag that will end up at the back of a cupboard. This chapter runs through how to use the patterns in the book, giving advice on reading patterns and understanding sewing instructions, with some helpful fabric preparation and cutting tips. Then at the end of this chapter you'll find information on how you can modify the size of bag patterns, which is one of the first steps to making bags the way you want them.

Using Patterns

The patterns, found at the back of the book, are all full-size, which means there is no need to hunt around the neighbourhood for a photocopier. Some of the bag projects have two or more pattern pieces (which are indicated on the pattern pieces), others have just one pattern piece and some projects simply use rectangles given as measurements within the project instructions.

1 Get a large sheet of suitable paper. I usually use pale tissue paper, but you can also use tracing paper, greaseproof paper or dressmaking paper. Iron the paper and the pattern sheet on a low setting.

2 Lay the paper over your chosen pattern piece and, using pins or sticky tape, secure the paper to the pattern so that it can't move around.

3 Take a soft leaded pencil (you don't want to rip holes in your paper with a hard pencil) and trace around your pattern shape. Also trace the various pattern markings, notches and darts if appropriate (see pages 18–19). See **Fig a**.

Fig a *Use a soft leaded pencil to trace the patterns and pattern markings to get nice easy-to-see outlines, and you'll avoid ripping the tracing paper.*

4 Lay out your traced pattern pieces onto your fabric. Align your pattern with the fabric's straight grain (see grain lines, page 19). If the pattern piece instructs you to place it on a fold, fold your fabric as shown in **Fig b**. Pay attention to the direction of your pattern – are the pattern pieces the right way up? Accordingly, is the pattern on your fabric also the right way up?

5 Pin your pattern pieces to your fabric and cut the fabric around the pattern shapes. See **Fig c**. Alternatively, you can pin your patterns to your fabric and then trace around the outline of your pattern pieces with disappearing marker or chalk to get an outline for fabric cutting. However, before you do any cutting, make sure you refer to the fabric cutting tips on page 21.

6 Transfer any pattern markings, notches or darts from the pattern piece to your fabric pieces using chalk or disappearing marker. See **Fig d**.

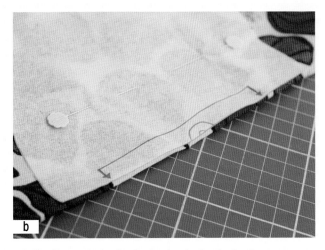

Fig b *To place a pattern piece on a fold, fold the fabric wrong sides together and position the fold line of the pattern onto the folded edge of the fabric.*

Fig c *I prefer to pin and cut around the pattern pieces because it's faster than tracing around the pattern and then cutting.*

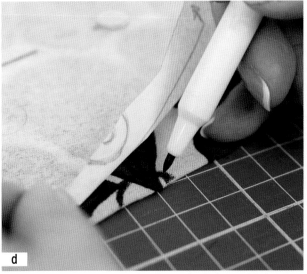

Fig d *While the pattern is still pinned to the fabric, transfer the various pattern markings onto the fabric.*

Label snob ...
Label your pattern pieces before and after using them; fold them carefully, and store in an envelope. Also store in the envelope any notes you make during bag construction, ready for next time.

Understanding Patterns

Besides the pattern shape, there is a variety of other information on the pattern pieces. This brief guide will help you understand what the terms mean and what they are for.

pattern piece name and standard information

seam allowance information

Language skills ...
You'll quickly become familiar with sewing terms and abbreviations. Keep referring back to these pages until you become confident.

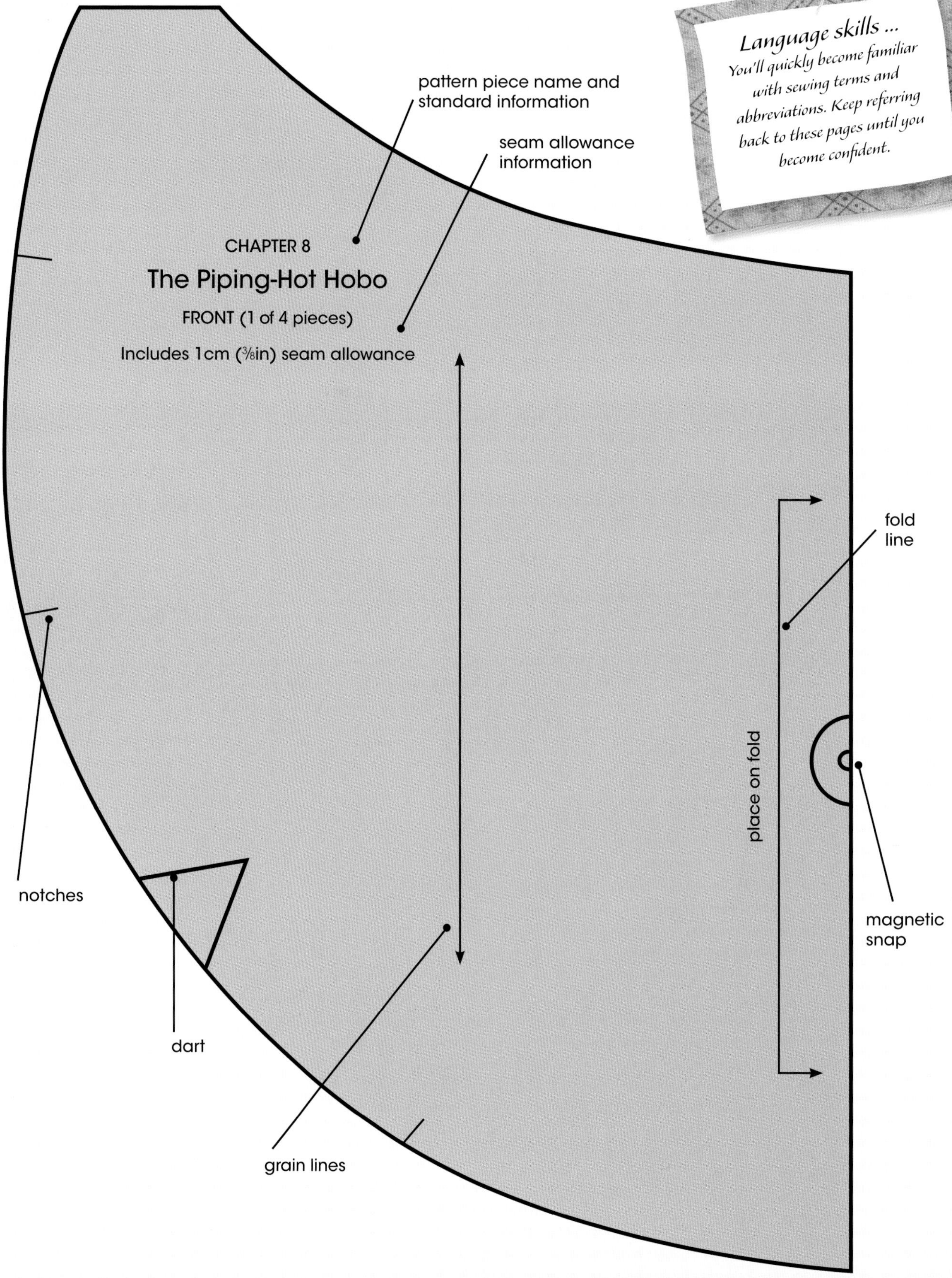

CHAPTER 8

The Piping-Hot Hobo

FRONT (1 of 4 pieces)

Includes 1cm (⅜in) seam allowance

fold line

place on fold

magnetic snap

notches

dart

grain lines

- **Seam allowance** – this is the distance between the edge of the fabric piece(s) and the sewing machine needle. So, if a pattern indicates that the seam allowance is 1cm (⅜in), you need to sew your stitches 1cm (⅜in) in from the edge of the fabric. A pattern should always state the seam allowance size and whether or not it has been included in the pattern.
- **Grain lines** – these are the two pointed arrows that help you to align the pattern piece with the straight grain of the fabric. The top arrow points to the top edge of the fabric and the bottom arrow points to the bottom edge of the fabric. The straight grain of the fabric runs parallel to the selvedge (the non-fraying edge of the fabric, which often has the company and fabric name printed on it).
- **Fold lines** – when a pattern piece says 'place on fold' you need to fold your fabric wrong sides together and place the appropriate edge of the pattern piece onto the fabric fold. In this way, the resulting cut fabric piece will be double the size; a mirror image joined at the fabric fold.

- **Notches** – these are the small vertical lines that appear on the pattern piece outline. These useful markings help you to match up seams and fabric edges accurately. Pattern pieces that need joining up will have corresponding notches. Transfer pattern notches to your fabric pieces using a disappearing marker or make small nicks with scissors.
- **Darts** – these appear as large triangle shapes that point into the pattern from the pattern outline. When fabric cutting, I usually cut these dart triangles out. For sewing darts see pages 48–49.
- **Other markings** – magnetic snap/twist lock/bag handle hook/zip pocket etc. markings need to be traced onto your patterns, and then transferred to your fabric pieces.

GLOSSARY OF TERMS AND ABBREVIATIONS

In addition to the patterns, you will also need to be able to follow the written instructions for each technique or project. The following terms are used throughout this book and in other commercial patterns.

- **Bag lining/bag exterior** – most bags have a lining and an exterior, which essentially means that most bags consist of two bags (the inside bag and the outside bag). Each bag is made separately before being joined together towards the end of construction. In this book I refer to the inside bag as the 'lining bag' and the outside bag as the 'exterior bag'.
- **Clip** – clipping your seam allowance helps seams lie flat when you turn your project right side out by reducing bulk in the seams (especially curved seams). For inward curves cut small V-shapes pointing towards the stitching along the seam allowance close, but not too close, to the stitching. For outward curves make small scissor nicks pointing towards the stitching (again, not too close to the stitching).
- **Clip corners** – snipping off the seam allowance reduces bulk in the seams of straight corners and makes for smoother and sharper corners on your bag when it is turned right side out. This results in neater rectangular pockets or fabric straps, for example. Before turning right side out, trim off the corner tips of your work close, but not too close, to the stitching.
- **Raw edges** – refers to the cut, unstitched and unfinished edges of fabric.
- **Sewing in a box formation** – particularly useful for stitching strap ends down securely onto your work.

Stitch the item in a box shape for extra strength and durability.
- **Topstitching** – a line of stitches that runs close and parallel to an edge on the right side of your work. The distance between the stitches and the edge will vary according to your preference or the instructions in the project. Topstitching is very useful in that it often serves both decorative and reinforcing functions.
- **Turning right side out** (sometimes abbreviated – TRSO) – simply means that you need to turn your (inside out) work the right way out. **Turning wrong side out** means the reverse of the above.
- **WS** – wrong side – the reverse or back of your work or fabric.
- **WST** – wrong sides together – bring two pieces of fabric together so that the wrong sides of the fabrics are touching each other.
- **WSO** – wrong side out – the wrong side of your work/fabric is facing outwards.
- **WSU** – wrong side up – the wrong side of your work/fabric is facing upwards.
- **RS** – right side – the good or the front side of your fabric or work.
- **RST** – as WST, but with the right side.
- **RSO** – as WSO, but with the right side.
- **RSU** – as WSU, but with the right side.

Fabric Preparation and Cutting

There's nothing like grabbing a few hours and making a start on a new sewing project. But before you rush in with your scissors it's worth taking a little time and care to prepare and cut your fabrics in a methodical way. The following tips and hints will help you speed up the cutting process and end up with a more professional-looking bag.

Fabric preparation tips

• If you want to wash your bags you will need to pre-wash your fabric to prevent the fabric from shrinking during washing. Put your fabric in a mesh bag to help prevent the raw edges fraying in the washing machine. (I don't pre-wash my fabrics because I don't think it's a good idea to wash bags. I prefer to 'spot wash' by dabbing the affected area with a moist cloth and a mild detergent.)

• Always iron your fabrics thoroughly before cutting. See **Fig a**.

Spray away ...
Rather than washing bags, try using fabric protector sprays on your fabrics to help repel dirt and block stains. Always read the instructions and test first.

a

Fig a *I know it's boring, but ironing is a necessary activity in all sewing projects. Always iron your fabrics thoroughly before pattern cutting.*

Fabric cutting tips

- Always cut on a flat surface and clear the decks before you get cutting.

- Speed things up by ironing fusible interfacing (if using) to the wrong side of fabrics before cutting out, see **Fig b**. See also page 37.

- Always use sharp scissors or a sharp rotary cutter for cutting out your fabrics. This will ensure that you get clean and accurate cuts every time. If you are using a rotary cutter ensure that you cut on a rotary cutting mat. See **Fig c**.

- Follow the grain lines on your patterns (see page 19) to ensure that fabric designs don't appear wonky.

- Try laying the fabrics and interlining pieces carefully on top of each other and then laying the pattern pieces on the top before pinning all layers and cutting. See **Fig d**. However, if your stacked up layers are too tall you will end up with very scruffy edges and your scissors won't be happy at having to cut through all of those layers. If this is the case, try layering your lining and exterior fabrics together and cutting, and then layer your interlinings together and cutting.

- If using fabrics with a directional pattern and you are layering your fabrics before cutting (as suggested above) be sure to check that your fabrics are the right way up. You don't want to end up with fabric pattern pieces with designs that are upside down.

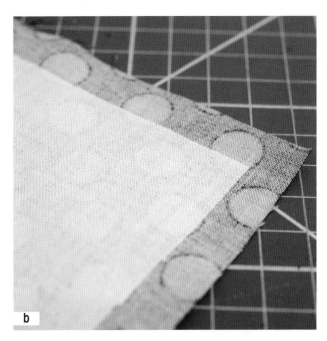

Fig b *Wherever possible iron fusible interfacing (if using) onto the WS of fabrics before pattern cutting. This saves the bother of having to match up and iron an interfacing pattern piece to the fabric pattern piece.*

Fig c *A rotary cutter makes cutting straight edges so much faster and neater. If you have a steady hand, a rotary cutter is great for curved edges too. Always use a rotary cutting mat – they not only protect your table, they also help keep the blade sharper for longer.*

Fig d *Another pattern cutting time-saving trick is to stack and pin the fabric and interfacing pieces on top of each other before cutting.*

Modifying Patterns

If you are a sewing 'newbie' the thought of deviating from a pattern may seem like a crazy thing to do, but it's actually very easy to make pattern modifications to suit you (or your outfit!). In their simplest form, bags are a front, a back and a couple of handles. But you can jazz up even a basic bag by changing its size, adding a pocket, inserting a zip or a snap, changing the handles or adding a couple of darts for volume, for example. Below you will find guidance on changing the size of the bag as the first step to modifying a pattern, but the rest of this book will show you how to change everything else – so read on. Because bag making is less complicated than dressmaking you'll find that it's far more forgiving if you haven't quite got the measurements 100 per cent right. In fact, half the fun of bag making is that you can often make it up as you go along. I do it all the time!

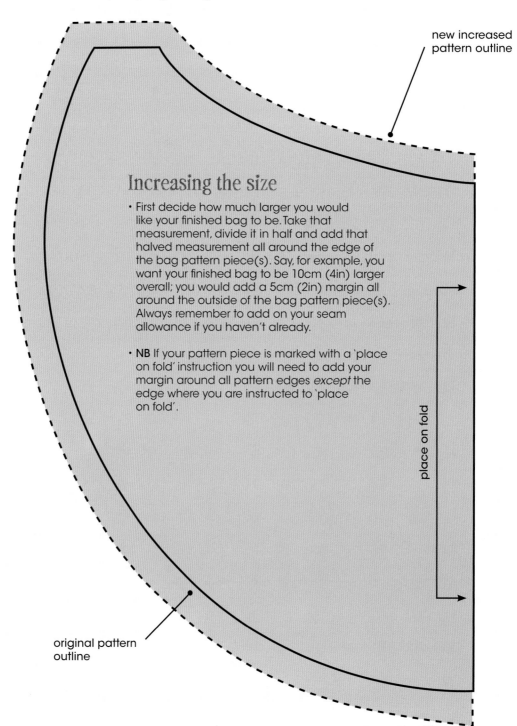

new increased pattern outline

Increasing the size

- First decide how much larger you would like your finished bag to be. Take that measurement, divide it in half and add that halved measurement all around the edge of the bag pattern piece(s). Say, for example, you want your finished bag to be 10cm (4in) larger overall; you would add a 5cm (2in) margin all around the outside of the bag pattern piece(s). Always remember to add on your seam allowance if you haven't already.

- **NB** If your pattern piece is marked with a 'place on fold' instruction you will need to add your margin around all pattern edges *except* the edge where you are instructed to 'place on fold'.

place on fold

original pattern outline

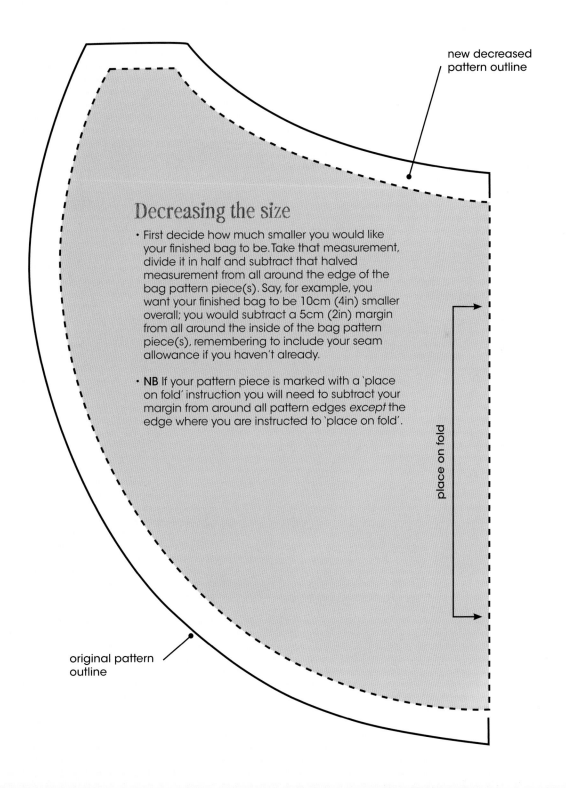

new decreased
pattern outline

Decreasing the size

- First decide how much smaller you would like your finished bag to be. Take that measurement, divide it in half and subtract that halved measurement from all around the edge of the bag pattern piece(s). Say, for example, you want your finished bag to be 10cm (4in) smaller overall; you would subtract a 5cm (2in) margin from all around the inside of the bag pattern piece(s), remembering to include your seam allowance if you haven't already.

- **NB** If your pattern piece is marked with a 'place on fold' instruction you will need to subtract your margin from around all pattern edges *except* the edge where you are instructed to 'place on fold'.

place on fold

original pattern
outline

Make it...
The Versatile Book Bag

Here we have three different versions of a basic book bag shape. I bet you can't stop at one! Master these simple totes and with the help of this book you'll soon be adding your own cool features like zip pockets, darts and fancy fasteners.

Easy as Pie *Pretty fabrics really lift the basic design of this bag.*

Flat-Bottomed Girl *It's quick and easy to pop a flat bottom into a bag, and your bag will look that bit more professional.*

Peek-a-Boo Pleats *Insert a bright fabric into the pleat to make eye-catching peek-a-boo pleats.*

NEED TO KNOW

- As these bags are unlined you might prefer to use fabrics that are the same colour on both sides (self-coloured) such as canvas or linen.

- All seam allowances are 1cm (⅜in) unless stated otherwise.

- There are no patterns for these bags as all you need are fabric rectangles. Fabric measurements are given in the instructions.

EASY AS PIE & FLAT-BOTTOMED GIRL

The super handy easy-as-pie tote bag is about as basic as can be but that's no reason for it not to look pretty. Whip up a few in under an hour for emergency presents. Jazz them up by playing with your fabric choices, use posh handles, or try adding a fabric flower. Our flat-bottomed girl is almost the same as the Easy as Pie bag except it has a flat bottom. A flat bottom is so easy to insert, gives the bag some 3D shape, and helps prevent your stuff from getting squashed at the bottom of your bag.

You will need

For each bag

- 1 piece of canvas or linen fabric for exterior, 50cm (½yd) x 112cm (44in) wide
- 1 piece of contrasting medium-weight fabric for bottom panel and straps, 50cm (½yd) x 112cm (44in) wide
- Sewing threads to match the fabrics
- Disappearing marker

Preparation

Cut the fabric pieces as follows:

Main body panel pattern = 81 x 35cm (32 x 13¾in) – cut:
- 1 x exterior fabric

Bottom panel pattern = 35cm (13¾in) square – cut:
- 1 x contrast fabric

Also cut:
- 2 strips of contrast fabric, 68 x 10cm (26¾ x 4in), for the bag straps

Assemble Easy as Pie

1 **Stitch the bottom panel to the exterior main body panel** – take the bottom panel WSU, fold in both short edges 1cm (⅜in) to the WS and iron the folds. Lay the bottom panel RSU onto the centre of the RS of the main body panel and match up the side edges. Check that the short edges of the bottom panel are lying at right angles to the side edges and pin. Stitch the bottom panel to the main body panel by topstitching along the short edges of the bottom panel. See **Fig a**.

2 **Stitch the long raw edges** – stitch along both long raw edges with a zigzag stitch that's wide in width and short in length to prevent the raw edges from fraying.

3 **Stitch the bag** – fold the bag in half widthways RST. Match all edges, pin and stitch along the side edges of the bag. Iron the bag.

a

Fig a *Ensure that the short edges of the bottom panel are nice and straight on the main panel; you don't want the bottom panel to look wonky on your finished bag.*

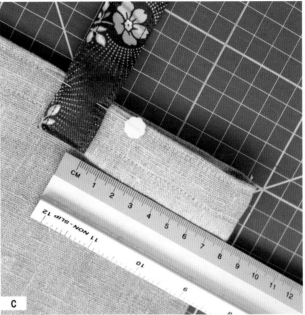

Fig b *Topstitch all around the bottom and top edge of the bag band.*

Fig c *Measure and mark the strap end position on the bag, and pin and stitch the strap in place through all bag layers.*

4 Fold and stitch the top edge band – with the bag still WSO, fold down the raw top edge 1.5cm (½in) to the WS of the bag and iron the fold. Fold down another 2cm (¾in) in the same way, iron and pin. Topstitch all around the top and bottom edges of the band ensuring you stitch though all layers 3mm (⅛in) from the edges. See **Fig b**. Turn the bag RSO and iron.

5 Make up the straps and stitch them to the bag – take the bag strap fabric pieces and follow the steps on page 103 to make two closed-end straps. On the RS of the bag, measure and mark 8cm (3⅛in) in from both side seams and 2.5cm (1in) down from the top edge. Place the outer bottom corner of one of the strap ends onto one of the marks you have just made. Pin the strap end in position and stitch to the bag in a box formation for strength (see tip). See **Fig c**. Repeat with the other strap end and then with the other bag strap.

Box clever ...
To sew a smart-looking box remember to leave the needle in the down position when you reach the end of a line. That way you can turn a perfect 90-degree angle by pivoting your work around the needle.

Assemble Flat-Bottomed Girl

1 Cut the fabric and stitch the bag together – cut the pattern pieces exactly as listed for the Easy as Pie bag and stitch together following steps 1–4 of that bag (opposite and above).

2 Insert a flat bottom into the bag – with the bag WSO, follow steps 2–4 on pages 54–55 to insert a flat bottom. From the tip of the triangle measure and mark 2.5cm (1in) on the seam for the bag bottom depth.

3 Make and apply the bag straps – following step 5 of the Easy as Pie bag (above).

Happy handles ...
Instead of making fabric straps and sewing them to the bag, you could buy ready-made handles and rivet them on. If riveting handles to the bag, reinforce the handle area with fusible interfacing (see page 36).

PEEK-A-BOO PLEATS

This version of the versatile book bag has an attractive but easy-to-insert pleat down the centre of the bag. As a bonus, insert a colourful strip of fabric inside the pleat to make pretty peek-a-boo pleats.

You will need

- 1 piece of canvas or linen fabric for exterior, 50cm (½yd) x 112cm (44in) wide
- 1 piece of contrasting medium-weight fabric for insert and straps, 50cm (½yd) x 112cm (44in) wide
- Sewing threads to match the fabrics
- Disappearing marker

Preparation

Cut the fabric pieces as follows:

Main body panel pattern = 80 x 50cm (31½ x 19½in) – cut:
- 1 x exterior fabric

Also cut:
- 1 piece of contrast fabric, 80 x 19cm (31½ x 7½in), for the pleat insert panel
- 2 strips of contrast fabric, 68.5 x 10cm (27 x 4in), for the bag straps

Assemble the bag

1 **Stitch the pleat insert panel to the main body panel** – take the pleat insert panel WSU, fold in both long edges 1cm (⅜in) to the WS and iron the folds. Lay the pleat insert panel RSU down the centre of the RS of the main body panel and match up the raw short edges. Pin and stitch the pleat insert panel to the main body panel by topstitching along both long edges of the pleat insert panel 3mm (⅛in) from the edge. See **Fig d1**. Fold the bag along the long edges of the pleat insert, iron the folds and topstitch the folds in place 3mm (⅛in) from the edge on the main body fabric side. See **Fig d2**. Stitch along both short edges of the main body panel with a zigzag stitch that's wide in width and short in length to prevent the raw edges from fraying.

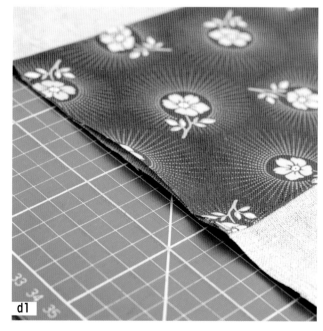

d1

Fig d1 *Check that the pleat insert panel is perfectly central down the entire length of the main body panel.*

d2

e

Fig d2 *Topstitching the pleat edge in this way will ensure the pleats remain permanently folded along the sides.*

Fig e *Stitch a dense line of zigzag stitches to anchor the pleats. Try using contrasting thread for added interest.*

2 **Fold and stitch the pleat into the bag** – at the top edge of the bag find the centre of the pleat insert panel and mark. Bring both side edges of the pleat insert into the centre mark, fold and iron in place. Stitch the pleats in place along the top edge with a 5mm (³⁄₁₆in) seam allowance. On the RS of the bag measure and mark 2.5cm (1in) down from the pleat top edge. Stitch a 5mm (³⁄₁₆in) line of zigzag stitches (in forward and reverse) to anchor the pleats on the front of the bag. See **Fig e**. Repeat for the other side.

3 **Stitch the bag** – following steps 2–3 of the Easy as Pie bag (page 26).

4 **Fold and stitch the top edge band** – with the bag still WSO fold down the raw top edge of the bag 2cm (¾in) to the WS and iron the fold. Topstitch all around the top and bottom edge of the bag band 3mm (⅛in) from the edges. Turn the bag RSO and iron.

5 **Make and apply the bag straps** – following step 5 of the Easy as Pie bag (page 27).

Left *For maximum effect use an insert fabric that contrasts with the main fabric for real 'pop'!*

2: CHOOSING FABRICS

Fabric is colour, texture, picture and pattern just waiting to be mixed up, cut up and stitched up into something amazing. The first part of this chapter explores different types of fabrics suitable for bag making, then suggests fabric sources, and finally looks at ways of working with colour, pattern and texture. The second part of the chapter talks about interfacing and interlining (also known as stabilizer). Mysterious and boring in equal measure, interfacing/interlining is nonetheless an essential component in bag making. We'll look at varieties of interfacing and interlinings and their applications, but first here are some of my tried-and-tested fabric and interfacing combinations for use in commonly made bag types.

Above There is something so gorgeously addictive about fabric. Collecting it is as much fun as sewing with it. Seeing my own fabric stash neatly stacked in colourful bundles gives me a warm happy feeling inside!

BAG TYPE AND DESCRIPTION	BAG FABRIC SUGGESTIONS	INTERFACING/INTERLINING
Messenger bag: soft structure, mid to large size shoulder bag.	Denim, linen, canvas, corduroy, upholstery/home dec weight fabrics with mid-weight cotton lining.	Woven fusible interfacing on all exterior parts and sew-in fleece/wadding in between lining and exterior.
Firm boxy clutch or medium large boxy bag: firm and can stand upright.	Quilt-weight cotton, satin or silk, faux or real suede or leather with silk or satin lining.	Medium fusible interfacing on all exterior parts then ultra-firm interfacing fused to exterior fabric with fleece sewn in between the lining and exterior.
Travel bag/large hold-all or padded laptop bag: boxy and upright.	Upholstery/home dec weight canvas, denim, heavy wool, corduroy, heavy velvet with quilt-weight cotton lining.	Firm fusible interfacing on all exterior parts, fleece and ultra-firm sew-in interlining in between lining and exterior.
Travel bag or large hold-all: soft and slouchy.	Upholstery/home dec weight canvas, corduroy, denim, heavy wool, heavy velvet with quilt-weight cotton lining.	Woven fusible interfacing on all exterior parts and fleece sewn in between lining and exterior.
Small or large hobo shoulder/across the body bag: soft and unstructured.	Quilt-weight cotton, heavy satin, upholstery/home dec weight canvas, denim, heavy wool, heavy velvet with quilt-weight cotton lining.	Woven fusible interfacing on all exterior parts and fleece sewn in between lining and exterior.
Bi/tri fold wallet: firm and semi-rigid.	Quilt-weight cotton, linen, canvas, denim with quilt-weight cotton lining.	Woven fusible interfacing and ultra-firm fusible interfacing on all exterior parts, and heavy sew-in interlining in between lining and exterior.
Jewellery/artist's/craft tool/make-up brush roll: soft, unstructured and padded.	Quilt-weight cotton, linen, canvas, heavy satin with satin/quilt-weight cotton lining.	Medium fusible interfacing on all exterior parts and fleece sewn in between the lining and exterior.
Zippered wristlet purse, pencil case: soft, unstructured and lightly padded.	Quilt-weight cotton, heavy satin, upholstery/home dec weight, denim, heavy wool, heavy velvet with quilt-weight cotton lining.	Woven fusible interfacing on all exterior parts and heavy sew-in interlining in between lining and exterior.

Feeling good ...
If you're not familiar with some of the fabric types and weights mentioned above, pop along to a fabric shop and have a good see and feel for yourself. Alternatively, many companies online supply samples free or for a small charge. It's worth getting to know how fabrics feel and handle.

Fabric Types

Broadly speaking, fabric falls into two main categories: dress weight (also known as fashion weight) and upholstery/curtain fabric (also known as home dec weight). As the names suggest, dress weight fabric is lighter weight and more suited to making clothes. Upholstery fabric on the other hand is heavier, more durable, and therefore more suitable for high wear and tear applications such as sofa covers and curtains. As bag makers we can use both dress and heavy weight fabrics to suit the bag that we are making. As a general rule, dress weight fabric is better suited to bag linings and upholstery weight fabric is better for bag exteriors, However, that is only a loose rule and there are clever interfacing tricks that you can apply to your fabric choices to override that rule (see pages 36–39). Meanwhile, here are some fabric suggestions that work a treat for bag making.

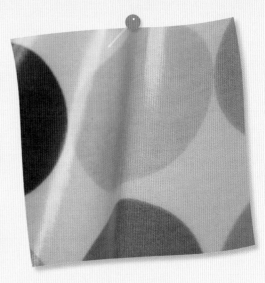

Oilcloth know-how ...
If you plan to sew oilcloth regularly, it is worth investing in non-stick sewing machine foot (see page 13). Also, be sure to use a jeans needle and only pin in the seam allowance otherwise you'll 'scar' the cloth with unsightly pin holes.

Oilcloth/laminated cloth Usually used for the exterior of bags, this vinyl-coated fabric comes in fantastic prints and has a tough waterproof surface, making it perfect for swim bags, travel bags and wash bags. The vinyl has a tendency to stick to the bed of your sewing machine making sewing with it quite awkward (see tip).

Linen This versatile, hardwearing and natural fabric is available in both dress and home dec weight. The linen that bag makers like to use is the natural biscuit-coloured home dec weight fabric. The colour of the undyed cloth with its attractive irregular weave makes it a great foil for embroidery and/or patterned fabrics.

Cotton/quilt fabric This type of fabric is used both in the lining and the exterior of bags. Cotton is available in many different weights, but for bag making try to use mid-weight cotton and up. Quilting fabric is usually made from cotton and comes in a fantastic array of colourful, beautiful and fun prints. You can use cotton for almost any type of bag.

Canvas/denim Usually used for the exterior of bags, canvas is available in different weights. Choose the heaviest weight that your sewing machine can cope with. Canvas is strong and it has rugged good looks. Be sure to use a jeans needle when sewing with canvas and denim. I think canvas looks best on larger bags such as shoppers, messenger bags, travel bags and beach bags.

Wool/suiting fabric Usually used for the exterior of bags, wool is fabulous for bag making. Wool is available in different weights, patterns and textures. Its incredible depth of colour and its yummy texture make wool a luxurious fabric to work with and use. Wool is hardwearing, but for bag making it usually requires interfacing of some kind. Wool has a more open weave so a strong dressmaking needle is sufficient. Try using wools for handbags, clutches and messenger bags.

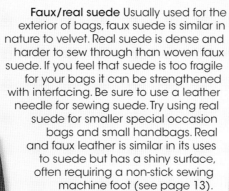

Velvet This is a luxury fabric that has fabulous depth of colour and a strokeable texture. The nicest velvet is made from cotton. Velvet is available in different weights – choose the heaviest weight that your sewing machine can cope with. Velvet frays easily so it's wise to sew with a wider seam allowance. If your velvet is quite thick or you will be sewing through a few layers use a jeans needle. Try using velvet for handbags, clutches and special occasion bags. Corduroy is similar to velvet in its uses and material qualities.

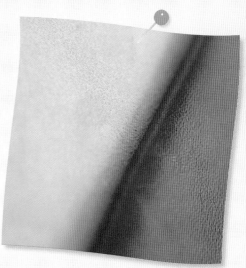

Faux/real suede Usually used for the exterior of bags, faux suede is similar in nature to velvet. Real suede is dense and harder to sew through than woven faux suede. If you feel that suede is too fragile for your bags it can be strengthened with interfacing. Be sure to use a leather needle for sewing suede. Try using real suede for smaller special occasion bags and small handbags. Real and faux leather is similar in its uses to suede but has a shiny surface, often requiring a non-stick sewing machine foot (see page 13).

Silk/satin Used both as the exterior or lining, silks and satins are luxury fabrics that have beautiful looks, texture and movement. Silk looks gorgeous pleated or gathered. Try to stick to heavier weight silk/satin because it's more durable and easier to sew with, while fine silk and satin are very slippery. Natural dupion silk is sturdy, has a lovely soft-sheen and an interesting texture from the small slubs in the fabric. Shimmery satin fabric makes a glamorous lining in an evening bag. Use a fine sewing machine needle when sewing with silk or satin. Try using silk or satin for any special occasion bags and purses.

Working with Colour and Pattern

Most bags require at least two different fabrics, one for the exterior and one for the lining. But how do you effectively combine the two (or more) fabrics? When it comes to sew-it-yourself there is no right or wrong, only what you like and don't like.

Playing with colour

For those of you who are new to sewing and don't know where to start when it comes to colour, here are my beginner-level suggestions for combining your fabrics.

Go complementary I admit I like to err on the brighter and louder side of things so I love nothing more than picking two colours that complement each other. Traditional complementary colour duos (hues that sit opposite each other on the colour wheel) include blue and yellow, red and blue, blue and pink, and turquoise and orange. If you aren't sure what colours complement each other look for a colour wheel on the Internet for reference.

Go tonal An easy way to group colours is to pick lighter or darker shades of your focus colour. Say, for example, your bag exterior fabric has a red rose pattern; your lining fabric could have pink tones.

USING TEXTURE

Combining different textures in a bag can have just as much impact as using different colours. Try pairing dissimilar textured fabrics with each other. The results will not only look great, they will feel lovely too. For example:

- Try pairing paring a velvet, wool, corduroy or suede bag exterior with a shimmery satin lining.
- Try appliquéing fluffy felt patches onto linen, denim or canvas.
- Try plaiting strips of silk to make bag handles for a real or faux leather or suede bag.
- Try adding silk or satin piping to a cotton or linen bag.

Go monochrome … with a twist Black and white is a classic colour combination, which always looks fabulous. Try adding a third flash of colour such as red, electric blue or lime to the monochrome palate to add an unexpected zing to your bag.

Playing with pattern

Patterned fabrics can be the hardest to know how to combine. There is no right or wrong – go with whatever you like, but here are some quick ideas to try.

Clashing patterns Provided the colours 'go' with each other you can have fun clashing different patterned fabrics together. This floral print works well with this stripe as the colours of the two fabrics tie in with each other.

Sizing patterns Don't be afraid to use fabrics with large-scale patterns. You don't always need to have the whole part of a pattern showing on your bag. Try cropping off an interesting section of a large pattern to make smaller sized bags or use it for a trim on a larger bag for a different look.

Matching patterns If you'd like both of your exterior and lining fabrics to be patterned, try putting the smaller patterned fabric on the inside of your bag. The smaller pattern inside the bag will be easier on the eye when your bag is full of your bits and bobs.

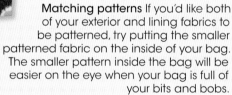

SOURCING FABRICS FOR BAG MAKING

There are lots of ways to get your mitts on bag-making fabric and not all of them require you to part with any cash. Here are some fabric sourcing ideas and shopping suggestions.

Upcycling/repurposing old fabrics Besides being good for our planet and kind to the wallet, repurposing is a way to elongate the life of items that we still love but can no longer use in their original capacity. Less-than-perfect items such as tablecloths, silk scarves, vintage dresses and curtains can be all reincarnated as original, creative and fun bags. Also hunt around for old bags and purses that can be taken apart for spares like bag handles, clasps, and other hardware – some of the vintage components are truly beautiful. Items for repurposing can be found everywhere, from your relative's attics to charity shops and jumble sales, to auction websites and even in newspaper adverts.

Shopping for new fabrics It's a sad fact that local haberdashery and fabric shops are shutting down at faster rate than they are opening up. I believe in supporting these shops whenever possible because they are often a wonderful source of inspiration and advice, and also there are times when you want to touch before you buy. However, many towns don't have them so thankfully there are loads of online stores stocked to the rafters with luscious fabrics. As long as you have a letterbox and a credit card you can feed your fabric addiction in just a few clicks ... oooh dangerous! Turn to the back of the book for my recommended fabric suppliers.

Interfacing and Interlining

Available off the roll in different weights and strengths, interfacing and interlining do look fairly boring, but hidden underneath that dull exterior lie some pretty amazing powers. Interfacing and interlining strengthen and reinforce fabrics and provide invisible support and structure to your bags, making them essential ingredients in bag making. This support makes bags more durable and therefore longer lasting and better quality. Without it most bags will look floppy and feel thin and unsubstantial.

From reinforcing soft silk to making cotton fabric stiff and boxy (for when you want bags to stand up by themselves) interfacing and interlining change the nature of fabrics giving you the flexibility to use nearly any fabrics you like to make bags.

What's the difference between interfacing and interlining?

Interfacings are typically fused to the back of fabrics. Most interfacings are fusible (also known as iron-on). Fusible interfacing has a layer of heat-activated adhesive on one side. The adhesive is activated by a combination of heat and steam from an iron. Simply lay it onto the wrong side of your fabric and iron it into place. Interfacing is particularly good for reinforcing fabrics, in other words making fabrics stiffer and stronger.

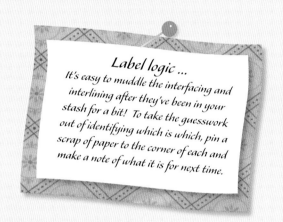

Label logic ...

It's easy to muddle the interfacing and interlining after they've been in your stash for a bit! To take the guesswork out of identifying which is which, pin a scrap of paper to the corner of each and make a note of what it is for next time.

Interlinings are usually layered between the exterior and the lining of bags. Interlining is soft and is typically sew-in (as opposed to fusible) and it is cut to the same shape as the fabric pattern piece(s). The interlining piece is paired with the fabric piece and both are treated as one layer during stitching, thus the interlining is applied by sewing it into the seams of your bag. Interlining is particularly good for adding support to bags by adding a layer of padding – perfect if fabrics are on the thin side and/or you want your bag to feel soft, plump and padded.

NEED TO KNOW

• When using fusible interfacing always choose an interfacing that is lighter in weight than your fabric. If you use interfacing that is too stiff for your fabric, the fabric will lose its natural drape and will become paper-like and therefore prone to creasing (just like paper).

• With sew-in interlining the weight-to-fabric ratio isn't nearly as important because creases in the interlining will not show up on your fabric.

• Product names for interfacing and interlinings differ from country to country. If you tell shop assistants that you are looking for a 'medium weight fusible interfacing', for example, that should be enough information for them to direct you to the product.

a

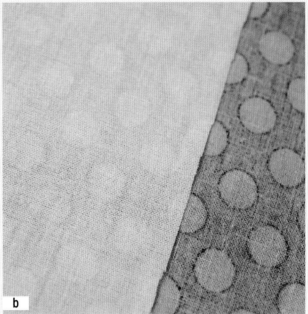

b

Fig a *The steam generated by the damp cloth (here I've used a checked tea towel) ensures a strong bond between the interfacing and the fabric.*

Fig b *There should be no creases or bubbles in your interfacing.*

Ironing on interfacing

1 Place the interfacing pattern piece shiny (adhesive) side down onto the WS of your fabric pattern piece, smooth down and carefully match up all edges. Place a clean damp cloth on top of the interfacing and set your iron to the interfacing manufacturer's recommended heat setting. See **Fig a**.

2 Applying moderate pressure to the interfacing and fabric, press the iron onto the interfacing through the damp cloth. Working from the centre to the outer edges, press each part of the interfacing for the manufacturer's recommend time until the interfacing is completely bonded to the fabric. See **Fig b**.

Sewing in interlining

1 Place the interlining pattern piece onto the WS of the fabric pattern piece, match up all edges and treat as one layer. Pin your fabric pieces RST (with interlining attached on the outerside).

2 Stitch the four-layered sandwich together with your preferred seam allowance. See **Fig c**.

c

Fig c *Stitching the interlining into the seams (along with the fabrics) will secure the interlining to the fabric.*

Weights of interfacing and interlining

Just like fabrics, interfacing and interlining are available in different weights. The thicker/stiffer the interfacing and interlining the more support they will provide. The trick is to combine the appropriate weight of interfacing/interlining with your choice of fabrics, and this will come with trial and error. However, the information here, along with the table on page 31, should help you to make informed choices and save you time and frustration.

Medium-weight fusible interfacing (woven and non-woven) Use with quilt-weight cotton, heavy silk/satin, medium-weight wool/synthetics and fine linen.

Heavyweight/firm fusible interfacing Use with upholstery weight fabrics, heavy linen, denim and heavy wool.

Heavyweight sew-in interlining Use in between the exterior and lining of your bags when you require only a little padding.

THE GREAT EXPERIMENT

I suggest you try my interfacing/interlining suggestions to save time, but do note that there are so many different fabrics out there and so many ways that you can combine them that the very best way to learn about which interfacing/interlining to use is to experiment – you may find the perfect product for your chosen fabric is not the one I have suggested. However, don't worry if you end up buying the wrong product because interfacing/interlining is so useful you'll be sure to use it on something else in the future.

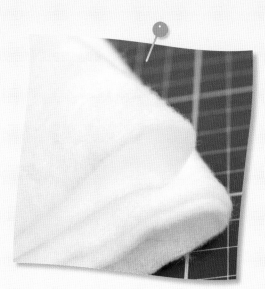

Sew-in fleece/wadding Use with any fabrics to add a more substantial padded and spongy feel.

Fusible fleece/wadding Use with any fabric that you want to add support and a light padding to. Great for silk/satins when you want to strengthen the fabric by adding support behind the fabric without making it at all crisp by using normal fusible interfacing. Very convenient to use as you can fuse it your fabrics. Great for all other fabrics when you want to strengthen/reinforce the fabric while retaining its drape (or fluidity).

Extra thick/ultra-firm/craft weight Available as fusible and sew-in varieties. Though it is extra firm it still has a degree of flexibility. It is perfect for adding a more rigid structure and boxier shape to your fabrics. When applied to or combined with your fabric this interfacing can make the fabric firm enough to stand upright.

STICK IT TO ME!

Another off-the-roll product is fusible web. This clever stuff is a heat-activated adhesive that looks like fine spider's web. It is used to bond two layers together.

Fusible web is neither interfacing nor interlining. You can use fusible web to bond your fabrics to your interfacing – this is very useful for example when your fusible interfacing isn't adhering to your fabrics properly or when you want your interfacing to be fusible on both sides. Fusible web is also brilliant for appliqué work.

Make it...
The Reversible Bucket Bag

Half the fun of making this cheerful bag is choosing three fabrics that all look fabulous together. Once you have chosen the fabrics you'll find this bag just kind of makes itself! The more you piece it together (like a colourful jigsaw) the more you'll want to see the yummy finished result. Pop a pretty fabric flower onto the button closure for an extra touch of cuteness.

Front view *A fabric flower embellished self-cover button with a brooch pin makes an eye-catching bag closure, and the pretty contrast binding does double duty – it binds the lining and the exterior bags together and it forms the bag handles too.*

Reversed *Fancy a change? Reverse the bag for a different look. Pin the button closure to whichever side you happen to be using today.*

Bottom view *For a smart and cohesive look use the same contrast fabric as the binding for the bag base.*

NEED TO KNOW

- Heavier weight fabrics for the exterior are not recommended; medium weight fabric is best because there will be quite a few layers to work with at the top edge of the bag.

- Choose three fabrics that are all the same weight.

- As long as you are consistent, it doesn't matter which fabric is interfaced with the fusible interfacing and which fabric is interfaced with the fusible fleece.

- All seam allowances are 1cm (⅜in) unless stated otherwise.

- Pattern pieces are given in the pull-out section and include the 1cm (⅜in) seam allowance.

You will need

- 1 piece of medium weight fabric for exterior, 50cm (½yd) x 112cm (44in) wide
- 1 piece of medium weight fabric for lining, 50cm (½yd) x 112cm (44in) wide
- 1 piece of medium weight fabric for contrast binding, base and button closure, 50cm (½yd) x 112cm (44in) wide
- Medium weight woven fusible interfacing, 50cm (½yd)
- Fusible fleece, 50cm (½yd)
- Sewing threads to match the fabrics
- 50mm bias tape maker
- 1 self-cover button, 4cm (1½in)
- 1 safety pin, 2cm (¾in)
- Disappearing marker

Preparation

Cut the fabric and interfacing pieces as follows:

From The Reversible Bucket Bag (main body) pattern piece (see pull-out section)

- 2 x exterior fabric
- 2 x lining fabric
- 2 x fusible fleece
- 2 x fusible interfacing

From The Reversible Bucket Bag (base) pattern piece (see pull-out section)

- 2 x contrast fabric
- 1 x fusible fleece
- 1 x fusible interfacing

Transfer all pattern notches and markings to the fabric with a disappearing marker

Also cut:

- 2 bias-cut strips of contrast fabric, 86 x 10cm (34 x 4in), for the side top edge trim and bag handles
- 2 bias-cut strips of contrast fabric, 29 x 10cm (11½ x 4in), for the centre top edge trim
- 1 strip of contrast fabric 30 x 6cm (12in x 2⅜in), for the button loop
- 2 pieces of fusible interfacing, 5cm (2in) square, for the button reinforcement

Funky fabrics ...
For a striking and graphic looking bag try this fabric combination – two different coloured plain fabrics with a contrasting bold plain or patterned fabric for the binding and base.

The binding, button loop, self-cover button and interfacing

1 **Make the binding** – take the four bias-cut contrast fabric strips and follow the instructions on page 141 to make your own bias binding.

2 **Make the button loop** – take the button loop contrast fabric and follow the steps on page 102 to make one open-end strap. With the short raw edges pointing upwards fold the strap in half widthways. Form a triangle tip at the bottom fold. Stitch the triangle tip in place (at the base of the triangle) onto the button loop. See **Fig a**.

3 **Make the self-cover button** – take a scrap of contrast fabric and follow the instructions on the pack to make the self-cover button. Decorate the self-cover button with a pretty fabric yo-yo flower if desired, following the product manufacturer's instructions (see page 147). Insert a pretty button in the middle and glue it to the self-cover button. Insert the safety pin though the shank of the self-cover button at the back and set aside.

a

Fig a *Flatten the tip at the bottom of the loop to form a neat triangle.*

4 Interface the fabric pieces – match the fusible interfacing pattern pieces to their partner exterior pattern pieces and iron them to the WS of the fabric pieces. Select a main body exterior piece to be the bag front and iron one of the button reinforcement squares to the WS centre, 4cm (1½in) down from the top edge. Repeat with the lining fabric pattern pieces, fusible fleece pattern pieces and button reinforcement square.

The bag exterior

5 Stitch the main body pieces together – bring the exterior main body pieces RST. Match all the edges, pin and stitch together at both side edges.

6 Stitch the base to the bag – bring the exterior base to the exterior bag RST. Match all edges and match the base notches to the notches on the bottom edge of the bag. Pin and stitch all around. See **Fig b**. If there is excess fabric at the curved edges of the base make small pleats at the curves and stitch through them – they will form attractive gathers at the sides (see page 50). Clip the curved edges. Turn RSO.

The bag lining

7 Make up the lining bag – make the lining bag in the same way as the exterior bag (steps 5 and 6).

Assembling the bag

8 Bring the lining bag and the exterior bag together – place the lining bag WSO into the exterior bag RSO. The wrong sides of the bags should now be touching each other. Neatly match the raw top edges of both bags and pin together all around, 4cm (1½in) down from the top edge. See **Fig c**.

The bag lining

9 Stitch the button loop to the bag – take the button loop RSU (with raw edges pointing upwards) and place it onto the centre top edge bag back (on the lining side). Match the top edges and stitch the loop to the bag (through all layers) with a 5mm (³⁄₁₆in) seam allowance.

10 Stitch the centre top edge binding to the bag – take one of the centre top edge trim bias binding strips and bind the centre top edge of the exterior bag front – see bound edges on pages 142–143 (except there are no overlapping edges to work with). Repeat with the other centre top edge binding piece and the back of the bag. On the back of the bag, lift up the button loop (so the triangle tip on the loop is pointing upwards) and stitch the loop in the up position to the top edge of the bag (through the binding) 3mm (⅛in) down from the edge. See **Fig d**.

Fig d Fold the button loop upwards and stitch in place to the binding.

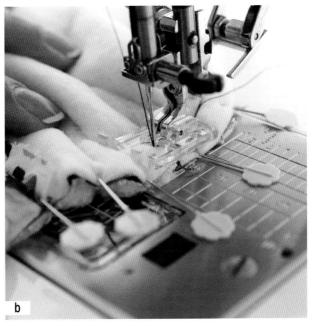

b

Fig b Pin and stitch on the bag side – it's easier than stitching on the base side.

c

Fig c Carefully match the top edges and pin the lining and exterior bag together 4cm (1½in) down from the top edge.

d

The side top edges and handles

11 **Bind the side top edges of the bag back** – take the side top edge bias-cut contrast fabric strip RSU and start binding the side top edges of the exterior bag back. See steps 1–2 of bound edges on pages 142–143 (and the rest of this step). Working from left to right start pinning and stitching the binding to the bag 5mm (³⁄₁₆in) to the left of the side seam. See **Fig e1**. When your binding stitches reach the top edge of the curved centre top edge, stop stitching and secure with several backstitches. Take the other end of the binding and pin and stitch it to the other side of the bag (begin 5mm / ³⁄₁₆in to the right of the side seam and work right to left).

12 **Complete the binding process** – see step 4 of bound edges on page 143 (and the rest of this step) to complete the binding as follows. Fold up the binding over the top edge of the bag and pin. From the points where the binding curves away from the top edge of the bag, fold the binding perfectly in half to form a bag handle. You may need to iron a new centre fold in the binding to do this. Pin the bag handle edges together. Topstitch the folded binding to the bag. Stitch over the curved top edge corners again to strengthen the base of the bag handles. See **Fig e2**.

13 **Bind the side top edges of the bag front** – bind the bag front in the same way as for the bag back except you need take the binding RSU and fold the short edges under to the WS 5mm (³⁄₁₆in) before you begin binding. Begin pinning and stitching the binding at the side seams – the folded short edges of the binding (at the side seams) should overlap the raw short edges of the binding from the back side of the bag. See **Fig f**.

14 **Finishing touches** – decide which bag side you prefer today and pin the button to the front of the bag.

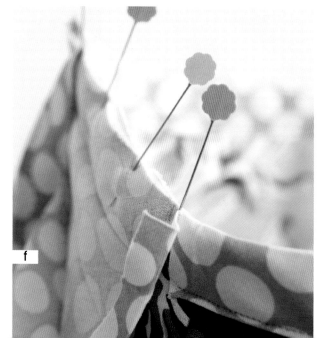

Fig f Place the short edges of the front binding over the top of the short edges of the back binding so they overlap.

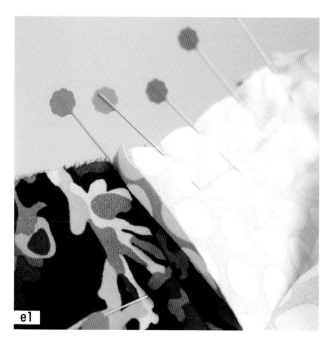

Fig e1 Begin pinning the binding to the top edge of the bag 5mm (³⁄₁₆in) before the side seam.

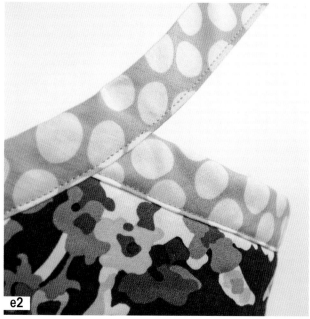

Fig e2 The topstitching along the side edge binding should flow smoothly into the bag handle. Topstitch again at the bag handle base to strengthen the stress area.

Right *Have fun chopping and changing your fabric choices to make completely different looking bags. Try making a petite version of this bag (see page 23) in deep coloured velvets and satins for a sweetly sophisticated evening bag. Or try inserting an easy-to-make slip pocket onto the bag (see page 124). The time to do this would be between steps 4 and 5 (page 43).*

3: STRUCTURE AND REINFORCEMENT

This chapter looks at various ways you can add 'va-va' volume and some exciting 3D shapeliness to your creations. It then looks at some ways you can reinforce your bags to help ensure that they keep their shape. In bag making, structure and reinforcement go hand in hand so it's important to have an understanding of both before you do any fabric cutting. The table below details different volume adding features (VAFs), their benefits, and suggestions for their use.

Turn up the volume ...
Any style of bag can benefit from some volume adding features. So it's time to step away from the pancake-flat tote bag and make some noise!

VOLUME ADDING FEATURES	BENEFITS	SUGGESTED USES
Darts: page 48	Quick and easy to apply. Does not require extra fabric. Versatile and neat in appearance.	Any size of purse or bag, from little coin purses to oversized bags. Also great on bag pockets.
Pleats: page 50	Decorative and versatile. Add one or several pleats to add interest as well as volume.	Any size of purse or bag, from little coin purses to oversized bags. Also great on bag pockets.
Gussets: page 52	The most effective way to add maximum depth and capacity.	Overnight bags, sports style bags, worn over the body satchels and hold-alls. Also great on bag pockets.
Flat Bottoms: page 54	A quick and effective way to add volume to the bottom of your bag and to flatten the bottom.	Any size of purse or bag, from little coin purses to oversized bags. Also great on bag pockets.
Gathers: page 56	Quick and easy to apply, decorative and versatile.	Many types of bags, pockets, wallet and journal tab closures. Also great on bag pockets.

Darts Adding a soft conical shape to wherever they are applied, darts look especially attractive on the bottom corners of curvy or rounded cornered bags. See pages 48–49.

Pleats An exciting way to add texture to your bags, the folds play with the light to create interesting shapes. Crisp folded pleats can look cute and preppy or they can look arty and structural, depending on fabric and placement. See pages 50–51.

Gussets Adding a gusset to your bag will effectively add side panels and will also a level off the bag bottom. A gusset is a great way of increasing the size of your bag without it appearing much bigger. See pages 52–53.

Flat Bottoms These are quick and super easy to insert into your bags. With a flat bottom your bag will have a nice 3D shape, will stand upright and your stuff won't roll around inside. See pages 54–55.

Gathers You could say that gathers are the more casual cousin to pleats because gathers don't require you to fold your fabric neatly and they give a softer, less-structured appearance. See page 56.

Darts

Darts are an easy way to add a small to medium amount of volume to your bags. They add a slight conical shape to wherever they are placed. Darts are usually placed on the bottom corners of bags, purses and pockets, and can be inserted onto curved or linear bag corners.

You will need
- Ruler

Testing times …
To see what your darts will look like on your bag, experiment with a piece of paper. Before fabric cutting, the golden rule is test, test and test again.

NEED TO KNOW

A dart begins life as a V-shape that juts out of the bag pattern outline (which always points in towards the middle of the pattern).

The length and angle of the dart are dictated by the pattern markings. The longer the lines and the wider the angle on the pattern is, the longer and pointier the dart is.

All seam allowances are 5mm (³⁄₁₆in) unless stated otherwise.

Sew your darts BEFORE you sew up your bag lining and BEFORE you sew up your bag exterior.

1 Decide on the dart position and draw the darts on the pattern – I tend to position my darts slap-bang onto the bottom corners of my bags. When drawing darts onto your bag pattern it's important that the darts are a symmetrical V-shape – the dart lines need to be the same length on either side. See **Fig a**.

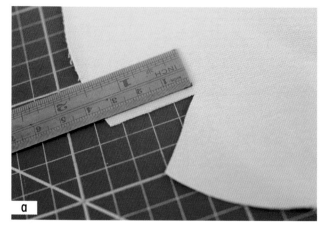

Fig a *The dart is symmetrical as both of the dart lines are of equal length.*

2 **Cut out the fabric and sew the darts** – cut the V-shape of the dart out of your fabric. Then fold the V-shape in half, RST carefully match the raw edges and hold in place with your fingers (or pin if you prefer). See **Fig b**. Stitch along the long raw edge of the dart with at least a 5mm (³⁄₁₆in) seam allowance. Repeat with the other darts.

3 **With the darts sewn, assemble the lining/exterior** – bring your bag lining/exterior pieces RST and when matching up the bottom and side edges pay attention to the dart lines to ensure that they match. See **Fig c**. After matching up your dart lines you can then match up the edges of the rest of the bag, pin and stitch the lining/exterior together. Continue with the construction of the rest of your bag (see page 156).

b

Fig b *Fold the dart in half and match up all the raw dart edges before stitching.*

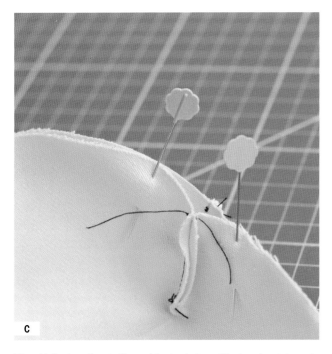

c

Fig c *Notice how the dart lines of the two halves of the bag flow into each other, making a highly professional-looking dart.*

Strength and beauty ...
When sewing darts into the bag exterior, team your exterior fabric with some sort of interlining or interfacing (see pages 36–39). This strengthens the dart and gives it a more attractive appearance.

Pleats

Pleats not only add volume to your bags, they also add a lot of visual interest giving you a great opportunity to play with your fabric choices and pleat position. If you think the look is right, you can add pleats to any bag or purse.

You will need

- Ruler
- Disappearing marker
- Extra contrast fabric if making peek-a-boo pleats (see page 28)
- Pressing cloth

NEED TO KNOW

- Pleating fabrics means building up layers, so unless you are sewing with fine fabric that needs stabilizing, choose a lighter weight interfacing or it will get too bulky for your sewing machine.

- Pleats can run from top to bottom, or you can choose to pleat just from the top of the bag and let your pleats flare out towards the bottom.

- When pattern making, remember to add width/length to your pattern piece(s) to accommodate your pleats.

- All seam allowances are 1cm (⅜in) unless stated otherwise.

- Insert your pleats BEFORE you assemble your bag exterior/ bag pockets.

1 **Decide on the pleat number and position and mark your pattern** – after deciding on the number, size and position of your pleats, mark the pleats on your bag pattern. I usually draw pleat notch markings on my pattern so I know where to fold my fabric concertina folds. See **Fig a**.

a1

Pleat practice ...
When deciding on the fold size and number of pleats, try experimenting with your paper patterns to see what looks right for the size of your bag.

a2

Fig a1–a2 *Make notch markings for your pleat folds so you know where to concertina fold the fabric ... like so.*

2 Decide if you want the pleats to run from top to bottom or just from the top of your bag – if you want the pleats to run from top to bottom add corresponding pleat notches (to those you made in step 1) to the bottom edge of your pattern. If you don't want the pleats to run to the bottom there's no need to make further changes to your pattern.

3 Cut out the fabric and fold your pleats – cut out the fabric pieces and transfer the pleat notch markings to your fabric. Using your notch markings as a guide, carefully fold the pleats and iron into place using a pressing cloth. See **Fig b**.

4 Stitch your pleats into place – sew a line of stitches about 5mm (³⁄₁₆in) from the top edge. If the pleats run from top to bottom sew a line of stitches along the bottom edge of the pleats too. See **Fig c**. Continue with the construction of the rest of your bag (see page 156)..

b

Fig b *Ironing the pleats will help them to stay in place and look crisp. Using a pressing cloth will protect your fabric from scorch marks and shininess. You can use any colourfast mid-weight cotton fabric as a pressing cloth.*

Sitting pretty ...
If you like you can insert strips of pretty fabrics inside your pleats to make scrummy peek-a-boo pleats. Full instructions for these can be found in The Versatile Book Bag project on page 28.

c

Fig c *Sewing a line of stitches along the top edge of your pleats will secure them in place while you get on with constructing the rest of your bag.*

Gussets

You can add gussets to flat or curved bottom bags – they are the most effective way to add the maximum amount of volume. While adding side panels to your bags, they also flatten the bottom too. One of the biggest pitfalls is that if you don't plan your pattern properly you'll find yourself with a dreaded twisted gusset. The simple secret to sewing a non-twisted gusset is to use plenty of notch markings.

You will need
- Disappearing marker
- Ruler

NEED TO KNOW

◉ To gauge the length of your gusset pattern, measure around the outline of your main bag body pattern pieces and add 10cm (4in). This leaves you with a 5cm (2in) margin for error on either short end of the gusset.

◉ If your gusset is longer than the width of your fabric you can sew two equal length strips of fabric together to make up the length. As the join will be on the bottom of your bag it won't be on show.

◉ All seam allowances are 1cm (⅜in) unless stated otherwise.

◉ Sew your gusset AFTER adding any pockets to your lining/exterior.

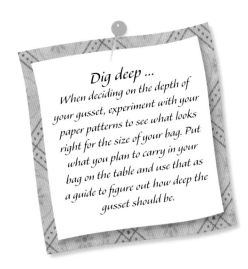

Dig deep ...
When deciding on the depth of your gusset, experiment with your paper patterns to see what looks right for the size of your bag. Put what you plan to carry in your bag on the table and use that as a guide to figure out how deep the gusset should be.

1 Make up the gusset pattern piece – decide on the depth of your gusset and add your seam allowance to your chosen depth. For example, if you want your gusset to be 8cm (3⅛in) wide and you are sewing with a seam allowance of 1cm (⅜in), the overall gusset pattern piece will be 10cm (4in) wide. When you have decided on the width of your gusset pattern, find the length of your gusset (see Need To Know).

Fig a1–a2 *Mark the centre of the bag gusset on both long edges and then add more notch markings on both long edges; make corresponding notch markings on your main bag body pattern.*

2 **Add corresponding notch marks to your gusset pattern and the main bag body pattern** – fold your bag gusset pattern in half widthways and with disappearing marker/chalk mark the centre on both long edges. Make a corresponding centre mark on the centre bottom edge of the main bag body pattern. Make more notch marks on your gusset pattern in the same way at equal intervals, remembering to put notch markings on both long edges of the gusset. Now add corresponding notch markings to the main bag body pattern as before. Adding notches up the bottom corners is usually sufficient, but you can also notch up the sides if you want to be extra safe. See **Fig a**. You are now ready to cut out your fabric pieces.

Less is more ...
It's a good idea to err on the conservative side when deciding on the depth of your gusset. If you overdo it on the gusset width your bag will jut out quite a distance from your body and will end up looking more like a box than a bag.

3 **Pin and stitch the gusset to one bag body piece** – bring the bag lining/exterior and bag lining/exterior gusset RST, carefully match up the raw edges paying extra attention to bringing the notch markings on the gusset and main bag body together so that they all correspond. Start pinning the gusset to the bag body piece at the bag bottom edge and work your way up the sides. See **Fig b**. You'll notice that the gusset is too long for the bag body piece (the extra length is there just in case things don't quite go to plan) – you can trim off the excess later. Repeat the process for the other side of the gusset and the other bag body fabric piece. When you have completely sewn the gusset to your lining/exterior trim off any excess fabric at the top of the gusset sides. Clip the curves (if appropriate) and iron the seams open. Continue with the construction of the rest of your bag (see page 156).

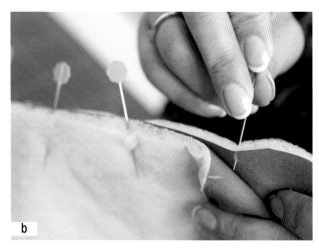

Fig b *Take the time to match up the notches on your gusset and the main bag body carefully and you'll sew a neat and non-twisted gusset.*

Flat Bottoms

Adding a flat bag bottom to a bag is as easy as pie. It's an instant way to add volume and a 3D shape to the bottom of your bags. This tutorial describes how to insert a flat bottom into a simple flat rectangle tote bag, but you can use this simple technique on lots of different bags, purses and wallets.

You will need

- Ruler or gridded cutting mat
- Disappearing marker
- Gridded bag bottom (optional – use if you want to reinforce the bottom of your bag – see page 57)
- Bag feet (optional – use if you want to protect the bottom of your bag form dirt and scrapes – see page 137)

NEED TO KNOW

● To determine the overall height of your pattern piece, add the finished bag height measurement to your bag bottom depth measurement, plus two lots of your chosen seam allowance.

● To determine the overall width of your pattern piece, add the finished width measurement to the depth measurement, plus two lots of seam allowance.

● All seam allowances are 1cm (⅜in) unless stated otherwise.

1 **Sew up your rectangle tote lining/exterior** – stitch your bag lining/exterior RST along the side and bottom edges.

2 **Flatten the bottom corner to make your bag bottom flat** – grab one of the bottom corners of the lining/exterior and match the side seam line with the bottom seam line (look into your bag to see if the side seam and the bottom seams meet and flow into each other). Completely flatten the bag corner to form a triangle and pin to secure. See **Fig a**.

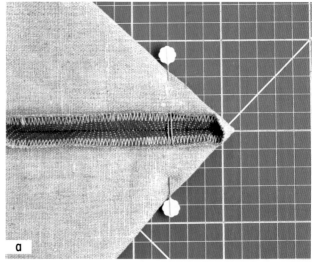

Fig a *Flatten the bag corner to make a triangle. Ensure the side seam lines up with the bottom seam.*

3 **Measure and mark your chosen flat bottom depth** – let's say, for example, you want your bag bottom to be 9cm (3½in) in depth. To make your bag bottom 9cm (3½in) deep, all you need to do is measure and mark a line that is 90 degrees to the side seam and is 9cm (3½in) long across the width of the triangle. A gridded cutting mat comes in very handy for this job. See **Fig b**.

Mock it up ...
To see what your flat bottom will look like on your bag, experiment with a piece of paper or your pattern.

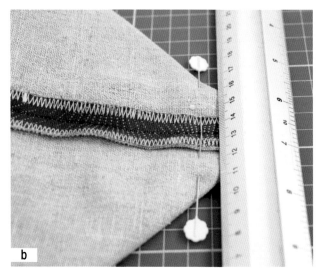

Fig b *Use a ruler or gridded cutting mat to ensure that the flat bottom side line is at a perfect right angle to the side seam and is your chosen flat bottom depth measurement in length, in this case 9cm (3½in) long.*

Fig c1–c2 *Stitch along the marked line and trim off the excess fabric from the triangle.*

4 **Stitch the flat bottom** – stitch along the flat bottom line mark you made in step 3. Be sure to sew securing stitches at both ends. To finish, trim off any excess fabric from the triangle, but not too close the seam. See **Fig c**.

Gathers

Gathers are a quick-and-easy way to add volume and to 'pretty up' your bags. The technique of gathering fabric is also used in making ruffles. Gathers are easier to work with and most effective worked in medium to lighter weight fabrics that lend themselves to a bit more coaxing and teasing.

Graceful gathers ...
When deciding on the size of your gathers try experimenting with your paper patterns to see what looks right for your bag. Don't cut the fabric more than double the width of the finished bag, as the gathers will look unwieldy.

You will need

- Disappearing marker
- Ruler

NEED TO KNOW

⬧ For big, puffy gathers measure double the amount of fabric to your chosen finished bag width/length. If you want the finished (gathered) width of your fabric to be 30cm (12in) you need to cut 60cm (24in). For softer, subtler gathers reduce the amount of fabric.

⬧ Gathers can run from top to bottom or you can choose to gather just from the top of the bag and let your gathers flare out towards the bottom.

⬧ All seam allowances are 5mm (³⁄₁₆in) unless stated otherwise.

1 **Decide on the width and position of your gathers on the pattern** – for example, are you going to gather the whole width of your bag or just the centre section? When you have decided on your gather width (and therefore your fabric width) mark your pattern with two points within which you want your gathers to appear.

2 **Decide if you want your gathers to run from top to bottom or just from the top of your pattern** – if you want them to run from top to bottom add two corresponding gather points (to those you made in step 1) to the bottom edge of your pattern. If you don't want your gathers to run to the bottom no further pattern changes are needed.

3 **Cut out the fabric and sew a line of running stitch across your gather fabric** – cut out your fabric and transfer the two gathering points onto your fabric. Set your sewing machine to the longest stitch and your bobbin to a very loose tension. Leaving long thread tails at beginning and end, stitch a line of straight stitches between the two gathering points without sewing securing stitches at either end. Pull on the bobbin thread (the bottom thread) to gather up your fabric to your chosen width. See **Fig a**. Distribute the fabric gathers evenly with your fingers. Set your machine to your normal stitch length and tension before sewing another line of stitches across the top of your gathers to secure them in place. Remove the loose stitch threads and discard. If your gathers run from top to bottom repeat for the bottom edge. Continue with the construction of the rest of your bag (see pages 156).

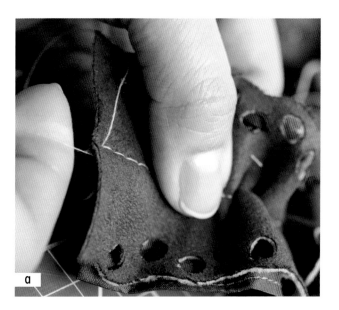

Fig a *A long stitch length and loose bobbin tension will enable you to pull on the bobbin thread to gather up the fabric.*

Reinforcement

We have just looked at various techniques for adding volume to bags, but in order for your volumized bags to retain their shape we often need to call in reinforcements. Bag making reinforcements come in the shape of certain other products and techniques. As we saw in Chapter 2, your number one defence against 'saggy bag' is interfacing and interlining, but sometimes you just want a bit more… Here are some products that you can use to further reinforce your bags:

Polyester boning This is a firm but flexible springy strip of nylon that is often used in corset making. Its flexible, stiffening properties make it perfect for adding support to side seams and bag openings. Sew directly into seam allowances to add a 'flexi-skeleton' to your bags. You can either sew the boning into one seam allowance layer, or right through both layers, or even one piece of boning on each layer of your seam allowance for super support. You will need to ensure your seam allowances are wide enough to accommodate the width of the boning. Also ensure that your boning is shorter than the length of your seam. Because polyester does not bend easily, the boning shouldn't wrap around your seams in a continuous strip.

Grid bag bottom This is easy to cut and shape and provides a durable flexible stiffness to the bottom or side panels of your bags. Never use a material like cardboard as a substitute because no matter how stiff the cardboard is it wont stand up to eventual wear and tear, plus cardboard isn't waterproof. This firm but flexible material will reinforce and give definition to your bag bottoms. You can also try it in the sides of bags for upright hold-alls, for example.

Fleece Also known as wadding or batting, this soft and spongy material is available off the roll either as a sew-in layer or fusible (see page 39). Fleece is brilliant for adding a soft and slightly squishy feel to your bags and I use it extensively. Fleece makes bags feel more substantial and in turn, better quality. Cut out the fleece along with your bag pattern pieces and use in between your exterior and lining. If you want a layer of support in your bag that is yielding rather than firm, a layer (or two) of fleece will do the job nicely.

Make it...
The Cocktail Ruffle Clutch

This purse shape is an enduring classic. Make one now and love it for years to come. The clean origami lines, slightly overlong width, and the fun ruffle combine to make the clutch look modern, grown-up and the right side of interesting. The body of the clutch is rigid, making it suitable to be worn tucked under your arm, or with its embellished chain handle the clutch looks just as good worn as a handbag. Perfect for an uptown lunch date, a city shopping spree or special night out.

Side view *This clutch has a nippy slimline profile.*

Bottom *The paper bag-style bottom folds not only look quietly cool, they add a little volume to the bag too.*

Handle *The optional chain handle has been embellished with matching silk from the clutch, adding to the 'expensive' look.*

NEED TO KNOW

- To make this clutch your sewing machine needs to have a free arm.
- A heavier fabric is best for the exterior of this bag because it is meant to be rigid. Faux or real suede/leather is best because it does not fray, which is important for the ruffle trim.
- Dupion silk or taffeta silk work best as the lining and trim in this clutch because they are more hardwearing and floppy silk/satin is not suitable for the ruffle.
- Use a jeans sewing machine needle when using heavy fabrics.
- All seam allowances are 1cm (⅜in) unless stated otherwise.
- Pattern pieces are given in the pull-out section and include the 1cm (⅜in) seam allowance.

You will need

- 1 piece of home dec fabric for exterior and ruffle trim 50cm (½yd) x 1.5m (1½yd) wide
- 1 piece of silk dupion fabric for lining and ruffle trim, 50cm (½yd) x 1.5m (1½yd)
- Ultra-firm fusible interfacing, 50cm (½yd)
- Single-sided fusible fleece, 50cm (½yd)
- Sewing threads to match the fabrics
- 1 purse chain with large links and spring hooks, approx 64cm (25in) long
- 2 D-rings, 12mm (½in)
- 2 magnetic snaps, 14mm (½in)
- Hand-sewing needle
- Disappearing marker
- Narrow double-sided tape, 3mm (⅛in)
- Knitting needle
- 10 small bulldog clips (optional – use instead of pins if your fabric is heavy)
- Hole punch, 4mm (⅛in)
- Wide wavy rotary cutter, ruler and cutting mat
- Cotton or linen pressing cloth

Preparation

Cut the fabric and interfacing pieces as follows:

From The Cocktail Ruffle Clutch (main body) pattern piece (see pull-out section)

- 2 x exterior fabric
- 2 x ultra-firm interfacing
- 2 x lining fabric
- 2 x fusible fleece

From The Cocktail Ruffle Clutch (flap) pattern piece (see pull-out section)

- 1 x exterior fabric
- 1 x ultra-firm fusible interfacing
- 1 x lining fabric
- 1 x fusible fleece

Transfer all pattern notches and markings to the fabric with a disappearing marker

Also cut:

- 1 piece of lining fabric, 24 x 15cm (9½ x 6in), for the inner pocket
- 1 piece of exterior fabric, 50 x 6cm (19½ x 2⅜in), for the ruffle trim
- 1 piece of lining fabric, 52 x 9cm (20½ x 3½in), for the ruffle trim
- 1 piece of lining fabric, 12 x 10cm (4¾ x 4in), for the handle loops
- 1 piece of lining fabric, 6 x 75cm (2⅜ x 29½in), for the purse chain trim
- 2 pieces of ultra-firm fusible interfacing, 2.5cm (1in) square, for the magnetic snap reinforcement
- 1 strip of ultra-firm fusible interfacing, 2.5 x 29cm (1 x 11½in), for the flap magnetic snap reinforcement

The handle

1 **Make up the handle loops** – take the handle loop fabric piece and follow the steps on page 102 to make one open-end strap. Divide the resulting strap into two equal lengths and thread a D-ring onto each of the handle loops. Set aside.

2 **Make up the purse chain trim** – take the purse chain trim fabric piece and follow the steps on page 103 to make one closed-end strap. Weave the strap in and out of the links of the purse chain. Fold each end over the end links of the chain and hand stitch down. Set aside.

The ruffle trim

3 **Make the top ruffle layer** – take the exterior ruffle trim fabric piece and using a wavy rotary cutter, cut a wavy edge along both long edges. See **Fig a**. On both long edges use a hole punch to make holes along the peaks and troughs of the waves.

a

Fig a *The wavy edge will give this ruffle even more 'oomph'.*

4 Make the bottom ruffle layer – take the lining ruffle trim fabric piece RSO, fold both long edges under by 5mm (³⁄₁₆in) and iron. Repeat and stitch the folds 3mm (⅛in) from the edge. Repeat for both short edges of the ruffle trim.

5 Combine the ruffle layers – lay the exterior ruffle trim RSU down the centre length of the lining ruffle trim RSU. There should be an even amount of lining ruffle peeking out from the top layer along both long edges. Sew a line of gathering stitches in the centre down the length of the ruffle as described on in step 3 page 56 except you will need to sew securing stitches at the start of your stitches. Set aside.

The bag exterior

6 Interface the exterior fabric pieces – trim off 12mm (½in) all around each of the ultra-firm interfacing exterior pieces to reduce bulk at the seams. Carefully lay the ultra-firm fusible interfacing pattern pieces onto the WS of the corresponding exterior fabric pattern pieces with an even 12mm (½in) fabric border all around and iron in place. Finally, iron the fusible fleece pattern pieces onto the WS of all of the exterior fabric pieces (directly onto the fusible interfacing).

7 Insert the magnetic snaps to the exterior front – insert the magnetic part of the snap to the RS of the exterior bag front at both magnetic snap pattern markings (see page 91).

8 Stitch the exterior pieces together – bring the exterior pieces RST, pin and stitch along the sides and bottom. As you sew take care to position the needle 2mm (¹⁄₁₆in) away from the edge of the ultra-firm interfacing. This will leave you with a seam allowance of 1cm (⅜in) and it will reduce bulk at the seams. See **Fig b**.

9 Sew the flat bottom – pinch one of the bottom (square cut-out) corners together. As you pinch you will notice that the corner will form what looks like a triangle with a 'sawn-off' tip. See **Fig c**. Neatly match up the raw edges of the sawn-off tip, hold securely in place with your fingers and stitch along the raw edge with a 1cm (⅜in) seam allowance. Cover your hand with an oven mitt or clean tea towel so you can get your hand inside the bag and use it as a mobile ironing board to iron the side and bottom seams open. Turn the exterior bag RSO. Iron the RS of the bag using a pressing cloth and your hand (clad in an oven mitt as before) to iron out the creases.

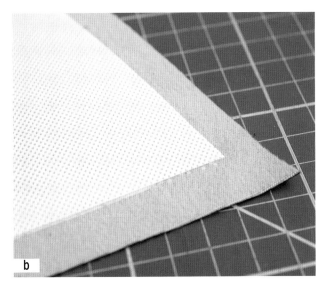

b

Fig b *Sewing a tiny distance away from the interfacing will result in neater-looking seams and will make turning out easier.*

c

Fig c *Pinch the square cut-out together like so.*

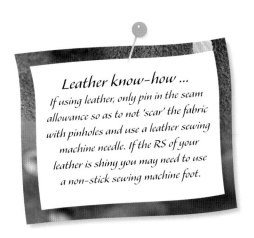

Leather know-how ...
If using leather, only pin in the seam allowance so as to not 'scar' the fabric with pinholes and use a leather sewing machine needle. If the RS of your leather is shiny you may need to use a non-stick sewing machine foot.

10 Crease and topstitch the paper bag-style bottom – using a disappearing marker measure and mark 1.5cm (½in) at regular intervals on either side and parallel to the bag bottom seam line. Use your fingers to pinch along the marks to form a bottom edge crease at either side of the bottom seam. You should now be able to squash the bottom of the clutch flat (and the bottom edge corners of the side seams will slope inwards towards the bottom seam). Lay the pressing cloth over the creases and steam iron them in place. Topstitch along both creases with a 3mm (⅛in) seam allowance through all layers. See **Fig d**.

11 Crease and iron the top edge of the exterior – with the exterior bag RSO fold the top edge of the exterior down 1cm (⅜in) to the WS. Iron the folded top edge to get a nice and sharp crease. See step 2 of drop-in lining method on page 72.

Fig d *See how the folds resemble a paper bag bottom?*

The bag lining

12 Insert a slip pocket into the lining – take the inner pocket fabric pieces and follow the steps on page 124 to make a slip pocket. Pin and stitch the pocket to the RS centre of the lining back fabric 3cm (1⅛in) down from the top edge.

13 Pin and stitch the lining bag together – assemble the lining as in steps 8 and 9 on page 61, but leave a gap of 15cm (6in) on the bottom edge of the lining for turning out.

14 Crease and topstitch the paper bag-style bottom in the lining – create the paper bag style bottom folds in the lining in the same way as in step 10 but do not turn the lining RSO. The creases are stitched into the WS of the lining.

15 Crease and iron the top edge of the lining – with the lining bag WSO fold the top edge of the lining down 1cm (⅜in) onto the WS. Iron the folded top edge to get a nice sharp crease. See step 1 of drop-in lining method on page 72.

The bag flap

16 Interface the flap lining – lay the fusible fleece pieces onto the WS of the corresponding lining pieces and iron in place.

17 Reinforce the magnetic snap area on the flap lining – lay the ultra-firm magnetic snap reinforcement strip onto the flap WS flap lining (directly onto the fleece). Position it in the centre 1.5cm (½in) up from the bottom edge of the fabric. Use a pressing cloth to iron it in place.

18 Insert the magnetic snaps to the flap lining – insert the non-magnetic part of the snap to the RS of the flap lining at both the magnetic snap pattern markings (see page 91).

19 Interface the flap exterior – trim off 12mm (½in) all around the bottom and side edges of the ultra-firm interfacing flap piece, then trim 6cm (2⅜in) off the top edge. Lay the trimmed ultra-firm interfacing piece onto the WS of the flap exterior, with an even 12mm (½in) border of fabric around the sides and bottom and iron in place.

Below *Experiment with contrasting shades for the ruffle, using different depths of the same colour as I have here, or use contrasting colours as shown in the steps.*

20 Pin and stitch the flap lining to the flap exterior – bring the flap lining and exterior pieces RST, pin and stitch around edges of the flap, but leave a 15cm (6in) gap in the top edge for turning out. Clip off the corners. Turn the flap RSO through the gap, smooth out, and use a fat knitting needle to push the corners out. Use a pressing cloth to iron the RS and WS of the flap. Finally, push the raw edges of the gap into the hole and iron the edges. Topstitch the flap all around the sides, top and bottom edges with a 3mm (⅛in) seam allowance, stitching the gap shut as you go.

Assembling the bag

21 Position the bag flap onto the bag exterior – apply a strip of narrow double-sided tape onto the WS of the flap 2cm (¾in) up from the top edge of the flap and peel off the backing strip. Place the narrower top edge of the flap RSO onto the flap placement pattern marking on the clutch back RS exterior and press firmly in place. See **Fig e**.

22 Stitch the bag flap to the bag exterior – stitch the flap to the exterior bag 5mm (³⁄₁₆in) from the edge the flap. Stitch another line of stitches 5mm (³⁄₁₆in) away from the previous line of stitches for extra strength. Remove the double-sided tape.

23 Pin the lining bag to the exterior bag – insert the lining bag WSO into the exterior bag RSO. The wrong sides of the exterior bag and the lining bag should now be touching each other. Neatly match up the folded top edges of the lining and the exterior bags and pin or bulldog clip together. Do not pin or clip around the side seams. See step 3 of drop-in lining method on page 73.

24 Stitch the lining bag to the exterior bag – with the bag flap folded down out of the way, begin stitching the lining and exterior bag together by topstitching all around the top of the bag with a 3mm (⅛in) seam allowance. As you approach the side seams, stop sewing and leave the needle in the down position. Take one of the handle loops (folded in half with D-ring attached) and insert it (with the D-ring pointing upwards) in between the lining and exterior. Tuck the handle loop down into the bag so there is only 1cm (⅜in) of loop peeking out. Hold the handle loop firmly in place with your fingers and resume topstitching (over the loop). Repeat with the other handle loop. See step 3 of drop-in lining method on page 73.

25 Finishing touches – take the ruffle trim and pull on the thread tail to gather up the ruffles so that it is the same length as the bottom edge of the bag flap. See **Fig f**. Space the gathers evenly with your fingers. Thread the hand-sewing needle with the thread tails and secure the gathering stitches at the back of the ruffle with several stitches. Hand sew the ruffle trim to the RS of the flap. Stitch through the ruffle bottom layer and the flap exterior fabric to sew several tiny stitches at regular intervals along the ruffle. See **Fig g** Clip the chain handle onto the D-rings of the handle loops and go find a party!

Fig e *Place the flap upside down onto the flap pattern marking on the exterior RS back of the clutch*

Fig f *Pull gently on the threads (so as to not snap them) and gather up the ruffles.*

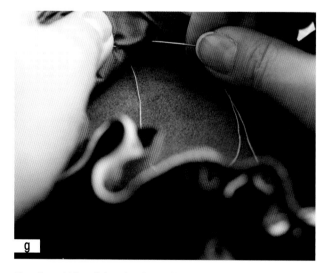

Fig g *To avoid the stitches showing on the lining side of the flap do not stitch through all layers.*

4: LININGS

While the exterior of your bag should be a visual treat, the lining of your bag should be just as delightful to look at and to use. As you read through this book and try your hand at some of the projects, you'll notice that linings are made from the same pattern as the bag exterior. You'll also notice that the process of assembling the lining together is almost identical to the process of assembling the exterior (with one or two exceptions, which are described in each project). With this in mind, this chapter isn't about how to construct linings because that is already covered in each project. Instead, it will look at how to make two types of zip inner pocket. It then looks at two different methods for inserting the lining into your bags.

Quick cuts ...
Because the lining is often cut from the same pattern as the exterior, you can save some time with clever cutting techniques (see page 21).

INNER POCKET TYPE	BENEFITS	SUGGESTED USES
Flush Zip Pocket: page 66	Versatile, useful and unobtrusive – keeps items safe and secure inside your bag. Can be decorative using a contrasting colour zip.	Mainly used in linings but can also be used on bag exterior.
Zip Partition Pocket: page 70	A clever pocket, which not only offers increased organization but also a secure zip-top edge.	Only used in linings. Great for folio cases, craft totes, day-tripper bags, or vanity cases.

LINING INSERTION METHOD	BENEFITS	SUGGESTED USES
Drop In: page 72	Creates minimum disturbance to the bag exterior. Lining can be shorter than exterior fabric to take the weight of bag contents.	Firm, rigid bags and those made from fragile or stretchy fabrics such as knitted wool and crochet.
Pull Through and Turn Out: page 74	Useful when bag handles are heavy because you don't need to hold the handles out of the way as you stitch the lining and the exterior together. Best for heavier bags as the lining and exterior are stitched together twice.	Softer structure bags and larger heavy-duty bags.

Flush Zip Pocket This is an eminently useful and easy-to-make pocket. Though this type of pocket is often found on a bag lining there's nothing stopping you from popping a zip pocket (or two) on the exterior of your bags too. See pages 66–69.

Line 'em up ...
The lining is another great excuse to introduce more colour and pattern to your bag, not to mention features such as pockets and zips.

Zip Partition Pocket This pocket belongs in the bag lining. Not only is it useful for adding a divider into your bag, the zippered top also means that this pocket can store your Holy Handbag Trinity: keys, money and phone. See pages 70–71.

Flush Zip Pocket

This is probably my most commonly used type of pocket because it's so useful. A flush zip pocket is the perfect solution for keeping important items safe. This style of pocket is usually placed up and away from the bottom of your bag.

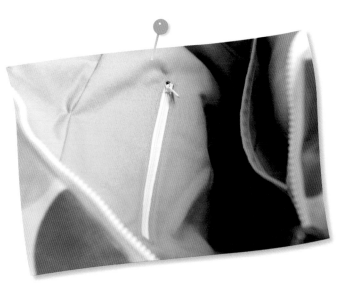

You will need

- Nylon all-purpose zip, at least 10cm (4in) shorter than the width of your pocket (see tip)
- 2 pieces of fabric for the pocket. To gauge the width and height of your pocket fabric pieces see Need To Know
- Ruler
- Hand-sewing needle
- Zipper sewing machine foot
- Seam ripper
- 6mm (¼in) double-sided tape
- Disappearing marker

NEED TO KNOW

- To gauge the width of your pocket fabric decide how wide you want your pocket to be and add two lots of seam allowance. The pocket fabric width should always be at least 8cm (3⅛in) longer than your zip.
- To gauge the height of your pocket fabric decide how high you want your pocket to be (measuring from the zip itself to the bottom edge of the pocket) and add 5cm (2in).
- All seam allowances are 1cm (⅜in) unless stated otherwise.
- Make up your pockets and stitch them to your bag fabric BEFORE constructing your bags.

1 Trim the zip – if your zip is too long, trim it to the desired length. Cut the zip from the zip pull side. Ensure that you leave at least a 2cm (¾in) clearance for the zip side seam allowance. See **Fig a**.

Fig a *Trim the zip to size from the zip pull end. Ensure that you leave a 2cm (¾in) clearance to the side of your cut for the zip side seam allowance.*

Cut down to size ...
It doesn't matter if your zip
is too long because it can
be trimmed to your desired
length (see step 1).

2 **Stitch the zip pull ends together** – take a hand-sewing
needle and hand stitch the zip pull ends together. See **Fig b**.

3 **Mark and make a hole for the zip** – take your zip and
measure the length of the zip teeth (not the length of the
zip itself). Now draw a rectangle as wide as your zip teeth by
1cm (⅜in) high onto the WS centre of one of the pocket fabric
pieces. This rectangle will be the hole for your zip and it needs
to be drawn at least 5cm (2in) down from the top edge of
your pocket fabric. Finally, in the middle of the rectangle draw
a centre line with a V-shape at both ends. See **Fig c**.

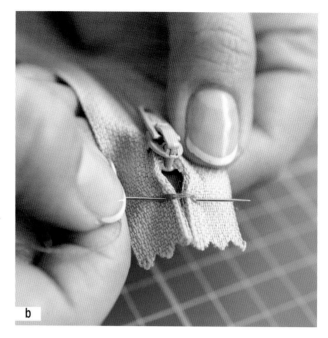

Fig b *Hand stitch the zip pull ends together for a professional-looking zip
– you don't have to be very neat as these hand stitches won't be on show.*

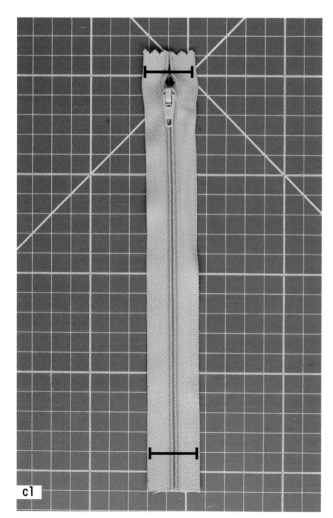

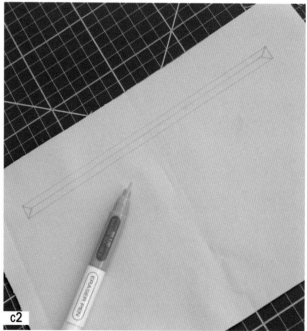

Fig c1–c2 *To gauge the width of the rectangle, measure the length
of the zip teeth (not the whole zip). The rectangular hole needs to be
drawn at least 5cm (2in) down from the top edge of pocket fabric.*

4 Stitch the pocket fabric piece to your bag fabric – place the pocket fabric WSU onto your bag fabric piece at least 7cm (2¾in) down from the top edge of your bag fabric to provide enough clearance for you to add internal fasteners (if using) and for you to sew your lining to your exterior at a later stage. Pin the pocket piece into position and stitch the pocket fabric to the bag fabric – stitch only on the rectangle. See **Fig d**.

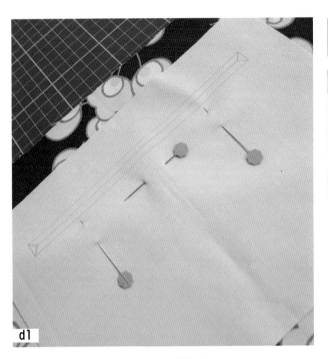

Fig d1–d2 *There is a clearance of 7cm (2¾in) between the top edge of the pocket fabric and the top edge of the bag fabric; stitch only along the rectangle outline.*

5 Cut the rectangular hole and feed the fabric through the hole – using the seam ripper make a small incision in the central line of the rectangle large enough for your scissors. You need to cut though both layers of the fabric. Cut along the entire length of the central line. Also cut along the V-shapes, but avoid cutting into the stitching of the outer rectangle. See **Fig e**.

Fig e *Cut along the central line. When you reach the V-shapes, cut into them as well, but don't get too close to the outer rectangle stitching.*

6 Feed the pocket fabric through the hole – pull the pocket fabric through the rectangular hole to the WS of the bag fabric (as if you are posting a fabric letter) See **Fig f**. Thoroughly iron the RS and the WS of the rectangular hole.

7 Stitch the zip to the bag fabric – apply a strip of double-sided tape to both long edges of the RS of the zip (so that the edges of the tape and the zip match) and peel off the backings. Take your bag fabric RSU and place the rectangular hole onto the zip. Manipulate the edges of the rectangle until it is lying evenly on the zip and the zip is positioned perfectly central within the rectangle. Press down to bond. Attach the zipper foot to your sewing machine and stitch all around the zip 2mm (1⁄16in) from the edge of the rectangle. See **Fig g**.

Fig f *Pull every piece of the pocket fabric through the rectangular hole.*

Fig g1–g2 *The zip is taped into a straight and even position inside the rectangle ready to be sewn to the bag fabric; stitch all along the edge of the rectangle to secure the zip to the bag fabric.*

8 Assemble the rest of the pocket – turn your bag fabric over so that the WS of the pocket and the zip is facing up. Place the remaining pocket fabric WSU onto the pocket piece (with zip attached). Fold the top edge of the bag fabric down out of the way so you can begin pinning and stitching along the top edge of the pocket. Pin and stitch all around the pocket. As you sew, ensure the bag fabric is kept out of the way to avoid stitching through it. See **Fig h**. The pocket is now complete.

Fig h *The pocket pieces are pinned together. The bag fabric is folded out of the way to avoid sewing through it while the pocket is stitched together.*

Zip Partition Pocket

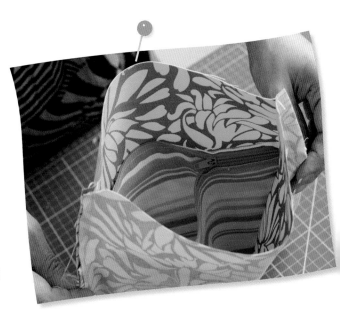

This inner pocket does double duty as a bag lining partition and as a secure top edge pocket. This type of pocket is only suitable for flat bags (or bags that are flat at the sides and have a flat bottom) so is no good for bags that have side panels or gussets. This style of pocket is usually placed up and away from the bottom of your bag.

You will need

- Nylon all purpose zip, at least 10cm (4in) shorter than the finished width of your bag
- 2 pieces of fabric for the pocket. To gauge the width and height of your pocket fabric pieces see Need To Know
- Ruler
- Hand-sewing needle
- Zipper sewing machine foot
- 6mm (¼in) double-sided tape
- Disappearing marker

NEED TO KNOW

◉ To gauge the width of your pocket fabric decide how wide you want your finished bag to be then add 10cm (4in). If you want your finished bag to be 28cm (11in) wide your pocket fabric will need to be 38cm (15in) wide.

◉ To gauge the height of your pocket fabric decide on the finished height of your pocket, multiply the measurement by two, and add 2cm (¾in). If you want the final height of your pocket to be 15cm (6in) high, your pocket fabric needs to be 32cm (12½in) high.

◉ All seam allowances are 1cm (⅜in) unless stated otherwise.

◉ Make up your pockets and stitch them to your bag fabric BEFORE constructing your bags.

1 Trim the zip to the desired length and stitch the zip pull ends together – following steps 1–2 of flush zip pocket on pages 66–67.

2 Stitch the lining and the exterior pocket pieces – with RS facing out fold one of the pocket pieces in half by bringing the short edges together. Iron the folded edge. Repeat with the other pocket piece. Open both fabrics, bring RST, and pin at the centre crease. Measure and mark the hole for the zip teeth along the centre WS of the crease. See **Fig a**. Stitch along the crease line from the edge stopping at the zip teeth markings. Repeat from the other edge. Sew strong securing end stitches.

a

Fig a *Pin the two pocket pieces RST and make two marks along the centre of the crease for the zip hole.*

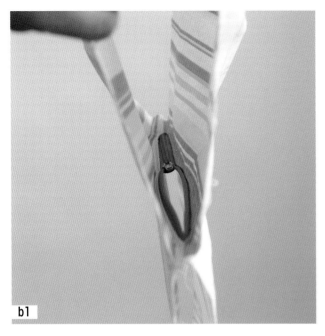

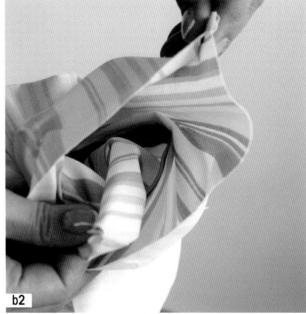

b1

b2

3 Turn pocket fabric RSO – flip the left top layer of the pocket over to the right and flip the bottom layer to the right. You should be left with the RS of both pocket fabric pieces facing out. Iron the folded edges of the zip hole to make nice sharp creases.

4 Stitch the zip to the bag fabric – following step 7 of flush zip pocket on page 69.

5 Stitch the short edges of the pocket – open the zip. Flip the layers over as in step 3 so that the WS are facing out. Pin and stitch both short edges of the pocket. Iron the seams open.

6 Turn the pocket RSO – hold the pocket up by one of the short edges so that you can see the zip RSU though the open sides. With your free hand reach in through the open side, grip the zip edge then pull the fabric down over the open zip. See **Fig b**. Rearrange the fabric pocket, smooth out bumps and iron. The pocket is now ready to be added to the lining.

Fig c1–c2 *Use plenty of pins to secure the pocket in position to the bag lining fabric piece; trim the excess pocket fabric from the side of the lining.*

Fig b1–b2 *Hold the pocket at the one of the short edges so that you can see the zip RSU in though the open sides; reach inside the open side o grab the zip and pull the fabric over your hand to turn the whole pocket RSO.*

7 Insert the pocket into your bag lining – just before you stitch your lining fabric pieces together, lay your pocket (with zip facing up) onto the RS of one of the bag lining pieces. Decide how far down you want the pocket to sit in your bag. I like to place my partition pockets at least 7cm (2¾in) down from the raw top edge of the lining (this leaves enough room for any top edge fasteners and for sewing the lining to the exterior at a later stage). Position the pocket centrally widthways on the lining fabric and pin securely to the lining. You'll see that the pocket is wider than the lining fabric piece – just in case! Bring the two lining pieces RST thus sandwiching the pocket in between the lining. Pin and stitch the lining. Trim off the excess pocket fabric from the side seams of the lining. See **Fig c**. You are ready to continue with the construction of the rest of your bag (see page 156).

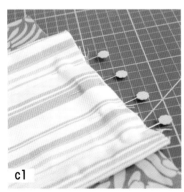

c1

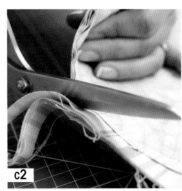

c2

Pocket width ...
The side seams of this pocket are sewn into the side seams of your lining. Therefore, the width of this pocket is the same as the width of your bag, plus 10cm (4in) (see Need To Know).

Inserting Linings: Drop-In Method

This method is particularly useful when your bags have a firm and rigid construction because it creates minimum disturbances (in other words less crunching and scrunching) to the firm exterior when stitching the lining and the exterior together. This method is also very useful if your lining is shorter in height than your bag exterior (see tip below).

You will need

- Your constructed bag lining
- Your constructed bag exterior
- Bag handles (if using)
- Pins or mini bulldog clips
- Cotton or linen pressing cloth

NEED TO KNOW

All seam allowances are 1cm (⅜in) unless stated otherwise. The seam allowance for the top edge of my bags is never less than this.

This method is a bit quicker than the pull-through method (see page 74), but it requires more accuracy because there is less room for error in your lining and exterior pattern cutting and seam allowances.

1 **Construct your bag lining** – insert any lining pockets (if using), stitch all around the bottom and side edges of your lining (do not leave any gaps in the seams). With the lining WSO fold down the top edge by your seam allowance (see Need To Know). See **Fig a**. Bring the folded edge to the WS of the lining and iron the fold using a pressing cloth.

Short and sweet ...
If your bag exterior is made from fabric that is fragile or prone to stretching (like knitted wool or crochet) a shorter lining will take the weight of your handbag essentials – thus avoiding the dreaded 'saggy bag'.

a

Fig a *Neatly fold the top edge of the lining down by your seam allowance.*

2 **Make up your bag exterior** – with the exterior RSO fold down the top edge by your seam allowance. Bring the folded edge to the WS of the exterior and iron the fold. See **Fig b**.

3 **Add the lining bag to the exterior bag and insert the bag handles** – place the lining in the bag exterior. The WS of the lining and the exterior should now be touching each other. Match up the folded top edges and side seams. Use pins or mini bulldog clips to hold the lining and the exterior together and begin topstitching all around the top of the bag. See **Fig c**. As you approach the side seams, stop sewing and leave the needle in the down position. Take one of the handle loops of your bag handles – if using (folded in half with D-ring or bag handle attached) and insert it (with the D-ring pointing upwards) in between the lining and exterior. Tuck the handle loop down into the bag as far as desired. Hold the handle loop firmly in place with your fingers and resume topstitching (over the loop). Repeat with the other handle loop and topstitch all round the top edge. See **Fig d**.

Fig b *Neatly fold the top edge of the exterior down to the RS by your chosen seam allowance.*

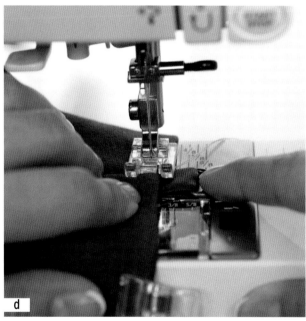

Fig c *Neatly match the top edges of the lining and the exterior. Clip/pin together and stitch all around the top.*

Fig d *Hold the handle loop in place at the side seam with your free hand as you stitch around the side seam of the bag. Slowly does it.*

Fray away ...
If you are working with fabric that frays easily, increase the size of your seam allowance when stitching the lining and exterior together. Remember to add on the extra seam allowance to your pattern.

Inserting Linings: Pull Through and Turn Out Method

This method is suited to soft structure bags and it is particularly useful when your bag handles are heavy. This is because the handles are attached to the bag in the 'down' position so they don't need supporting (or to be kept out of the way of your stitching) during bag construction.

You will need

- Your constructed bag lining
- Your constructed bag exterior
- Bag handles (if using)
- Pins or mini bulldog clips
- Cotton or linen pressing cloth

NEED TO KNOW

◉ All seam allowances are 1cm (⅜in) unless stated otherwise. The seam allowance for the top edge of my bags is never less than this (see also tip on page 73).

◉ This method takes a little longer than the drop-in method (see page 72), but it is more forgiving when it comes to fitting your lining and exterior together before pinning and stitching.

1 **Assemble the bag lining** – make up your bag lining (including adding any lining pockets if using). As you stitch your lining together leave a large enough gap in the bottom or side edge for turning out.

2 **Assemble the bag exterior** – make up your bag exterior. Turn your bag exterior RSO.

3 **Stitch the handles to the bag exterior** – with ready-made bag handles (if using) attached, stitch bag handle loops to the RS top edge of the bag exterior. The handle loops need to be pointing downwards. See pages 102 and 153. **Or attach handmade bag straps** (if using) to the bag exterior top edge. The bag straps need to be pointing downwards. See pages 102 and 151, step 4. See **Fig a**.

a

Fig a *Stitch your bag straps WSO into the RS top edge of the bag exterior.*

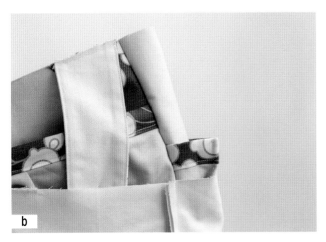

b

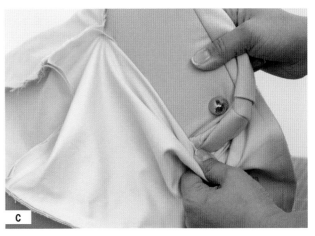

c

Fig b *Fully insert the exterior RSO into the lining WSO.*

Fig c *Gently pull the exterior bag out through the gap in the lining*

4 Add the lining to the exterior – place the bag exterior RSO into the bag lining WSO. The RS of the lining and the exterior should now be touching each other. Match top edges and side seams. See **Fig b**.

5 Pin the lining bag to the exterior bag – use pins or mini bulldog clips to hold the lining and the exterior together and stitch all round the top edge. Reach into the gap in the lining and pull the exterior bag out through the hole. See **Fig c**.

6 Replace the lining back in to the exterior – at the same time turn the lining RSO and push the lining into the emerging bag exterior. Stitch the gap in the lining shut by pushing the raw edge into the hole and topstitching the open edge. See **Fig d**. Smooth out any bumps and iron the bag using a pressing cloth.

7 Finishing touches (optional) – topstitch the top edge of the bag for extra strength and a neat and decorative finish.

Mystery movements ...
Even if you are precise with your pattern cutting and seam allowances, fabrics can stretch or move around – it's mysterious, but it happens! Using this method you can slightly stretch or squash the lining to fit if it is a less-than-perfect match.

d

Fig d *Neatly push the raw edges of the gap in the lining into the hole and topstitch it shut.*

Make it...
The Organized Office Bag

Perfect for guys or gals, this bag is a bit more special than the average messenger bag. Inside you'll find plenty of storage space, organizer pockets, and an optional harness to keep your precious laptop safely strapped against the back of the bag. The twist lock closures on the bag not only look really professional, they are safe for use with your laptop too. Whether you are taking it to work, college or the local coffee shop, this bag will look the business as much as you do!

Adjustable strap *Ensure you have ultimate comfort as you lug around your mobile office with a fully adjustable strap.*

Side view *The deep gusset provides lots of storage space for your laptop, notepads, document folders and lunch.*

Interior *Keep your stationery, keys, wallet and water bottle all organized in their own pockets. The adjustable harness will prevent your laptop from moving around inside the bag.*

NEED TO KNOW

- Medium to heavyweight fabric is best for this bag because it needs to be able to cope with heavy loads and provide protection for your computer and gadgets.

- In this bag the woven fusible interfacing is applied to the exterior fabric. The fusible fleece is applied to the lining fabric.

- All seam allowances are 1cm (⅜in) unless stated.

- Pattern pieces are given in the pull-out section and include the 1cm (⅜in) seam allowance.

You will need

- 1 piece of home dec fabric for exterior, 1m (1yd) x 137cm (54in) wide
- 1 piece of home dec fabric for lining, 1m (1yd) x 137cm (54in) wide
- Sewing threads to match the fabrics
- Medium-weight woven fusible interfacing, 1m (1yd)
- Fusible fleece, 1m (1yd)
- Ultra-firm fusible interfacing for flap and front main body reinforcement, 50cm (½yd)
- 2 rectangular rings, 4cm (1½in)
- 1 metal slider, 4cm (1½in) wide
- 2 D-rings, 4cm (1½in) (optional)
- All purpose zip, 30cm (12in)
- 1 piece of elastic, 18cm x 5mm (7 x ³⁄₁₆in)
- Seam ripper
- Pressing cloth
- Seam allowance guide (optional – see page 13)
- Disappearing marker

Preparation

Cut the fabric and interfacing pieces as follows:

From The Organized Office Bag (main body) pattern piece (see pull-out section)
- 2 x exterior fabric
- 2 x fusible interfacing
- 2 x lining fabric
- 2 x fusible fleece
- 1 x ultra-firm fusible interfacing (from the bottom half of the pattern – see pattern markings)

From The Organized Office Bag (flap) pattern piece (see pull-out section)
- 1 x exterior fabric
- 1 x fusible interfacing
- 1 x lining fabric
- 1 x fusible fleece
- 1 x ultra-firm fusible interfacing (from the bottom half of the pattern – see pattern markings)

Transfer all pattern notches and markings to the fabric with a disappearing marker

Also cut:
- 2 pieces each of lining and exterior fabric, 52 x 12cm (20½ x 4¾in), for the gusset
- 2 pieces each of woven fusible interfacing and fusible fleece, 52 x 12cm (20½ x 4¾in), for the gusset
- 2 pieces of lining fabric, 32 x 15cm (12½ x 6in), for the lining flush zip pocket
- 1 piece of lining fabric, 18 x 12cm (7 x 4¾in), for the lining penholder
- 2 pieces of lining fabric, 18cm (7in) square, for the elasticized-top pocket
- 1 strip of exterior fabric, 130 x 14cm (51 x 5¼in), for the handle loops and adjustable strap
- 2 pieces of lining fabric, 26 x 18cm (10¼ x 7in), for the laptop harness (optional)
- 1 strip of lining fabric, 30 x 14cm (12 x 5½in), for the laptop harness strap and loop (optional)

The interfacing, gusset, strap and laptop harness

1 **Interface the exterior flap and exterior main body front** – take the ultra-firm fusible interfacing pattern pieces and trim off 1.5cm (½in) from the side, bottom, and curved corner edges. Take the main body ultra-firm interfacing piece and place it onto the WS of the main body front fabric piece. Ensure there is a 1.5cm (½in) fabric margin all around the bottom and side edges of interfacing. Iron in place. Repeat with the flap ultra-firm interfacing and flap fabric piece.

2 **Interface the fabric pieces** – match the woven fusible interfacing pattern pieces to their partner exterior fabric pattern pieces and iron them to the WS of the fabric pieces. Iron the fusible fleece pattern pieces onto the WS of all of the lining fabric pieces.

3 **Stitch the gusset fabric pieces** – take the exterior gusset pieces RST, pin and stitch one of the short edges. Iron the seam open. Repeat with the gusset lining pieces. Open out the exterior gusset RSO to make one long strip and make notch marking on both long edges to match the notch markings on the bottom edge of the main pattern piece. Repeat with the lining gusset. See **Fig a**.

Fig a These notch markings will help later to ensure that you sew a straight (and untwisted) gusset to the bag.

4 **Make the handle loops** – take the handle loop/adjustable strap fabric and cut off a 16cm (6¼in) piece and follow the steps on page 102 to make one open-end strap. Divide the resulting strap into two equal lengths and thread a rectangular ring onto each of the handle loops.

5 **Make the adjustable strap** – take the remainder of the handle loop/adjustable strap fabric and follow the steps on page 103 to make one closed-end strap and set aside.

6 **Make the (optional) laptop harness loop and strap** – take the laptop harness strap and loop fabric and cut off a 20cm (8in) piece, then follow the steps on page 103 to make one closed-end strap. Take the remainder of the laptop harness strap and loop fabric and follow the steps on page 102 to make one open-end strap. Thread the two D-rings onto the harness loop.

7 **Make the (optional) laptop harness** – round off the top edge corners of the harness fabric pieces if desired. Place one of the short edges of the harness strap onto the centre top edge RS of one of the harness pieces. Match the edges, pin and stitch in place with a 5mm (³⁄₁₆in) seam allowance. Bring the harness fabric pieces RST, match all edges, pin and stitch along the top and side edges. Iron the seams open, clip the corners or curves as appropriate. Turn RSO and iron using a pressing cloth. See **Fig b**.

The bag exterior

8 **Insert the twist lock buttons** – follow step 2 on page 92 to insert the twist lock buttons to the bag exterior front at the twist lock markings.

9 **Stitch the exterior gusset to the exterior main body** – bring the bag exterior main body front and the exterior gusset pieces RST. Ensure the join on the gusset is positioned in the centre bottom edge of the bag exterior. Match the notch markings on the exterior gusset with the notches on the main body and pin and stitch together (on the gusset side) along the bottom and side edges (see pages 52–53). Clip the curved seams and iron the seams open. Repeat with the exterior back fabric and gusset, only this time pin and stitch on the main body side. Trim off the excess gusset fabric at both gusset top edges. See **Fig c**. Turn the bag RSO and iron using a pressing cloth.

10 **Pin and stitch the handle loops to the exterior gusset** – take one of the handle loops (folded in half with rectangular ring still attached) and place it onto the centre top edge of the exterior gusset piece. Match up the raw edges of the handle loop and the gusset. Hold the handle loop in place with your fingers and stitch to the RS bag exterior with a 5mm (³⁄₁₆in) seam allowance. See **Fig d**. Repeat with the other handle loop.

Fig b *One laptop harness and harness loop ready for stitching into the lining.*

Fig c *Cut of the excess fabric off both the short edges of the gusset. I always make my gussets too long, just in case.*

Fig d *Stitch the handle loop to the exterior gusset so the rectangular ring is pointing away from the edge of the fabric.*

The bag lining

11 **Make up the lining penholder** – take the penholder fabric piece and stitch a zigzag along one long edge and both short edges. With the penholder fabric piece RSU fold under the zigzag edges 1cm (⅜in) to the WS and iron the folds. Topstitch along the long folded (zigzag) edge 3mm (⅛in) away from the edge. Measure and mark three equidistant vertical lines on the penholder fabric for the penholder divider lines. See **Fig e**.

12 **Make up the elasticized-top lining pocket** – take the elasticized-top pocket fabric pieces and elastic and follow steps 1–4 on pages 128–129 to make an elasticized-top pocket, but do not stitch the pocket to the lining yet.

15 **Stitch the laptop harness and loop to the lining main body back** – if not making the laptop harness proceed to step 17. Take the other lining main body piece RSU (with no pockets) and position the bottom edge of the harness RSO onto the centre bottom edge of the main body lining fabric piece. Pin and stitch in place on the bottom edge with a 5mm (³⁄₁₆in) seam allowance. Take the folded harness loop with D-rings attached and place it onto the RS centre top edge of the bag main body lining fabric piece. Match up the raw edges of the harness loop and the bag lining fabric, pin and stitch in place with a 5mm (³⁄₁₆in) seam allowance.

16 **Stitch the lining gusset to the lining main body** – stitch in the same as way as for step 9, except leave a 15cm (6in) gap in the middle of one of the side edges for turning out.

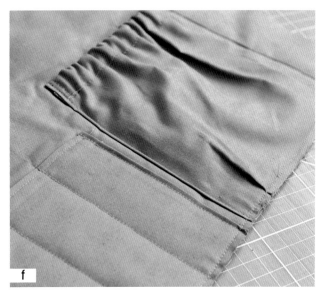

Fig e *Measure and mark the pocket divider lines on the lining pocket – be sure to use a disappearing marker!*

Fig f *Stitch the penholder and elasticized-top pocket side by side on the bottom edge of the main body lining.*

13 **Stitch the penholder and elasticized-top pocket to the lining main body front** – take one of the lining main body pieces RSU and position the penholder RSU 4cm (1½in) in from the side edge (to the left or right side of the main body fabric, as desired). Match the bottom edges of the lining main body and the penholder and pin. Stitch the penholder to the lining along the side edges and divider lines of the penholder. Repeat with the elasticized-top pocket and the opposite side of the main body lining fabric. See **Fig f**.

14 **Make up and insert the flush zip pocket** – take the two flush zip pocket fabric pieces and the zip and insert a flush zip pocket into the centre of the lining main body piece (with the penholder and elasticized-top pocket) 4cm (1½in) down from the top edge. See steps 2–8 of flush zip pocket on pages 67–69.

The bag flap

17 **Stitch the flap** – bring exterior flap and lining flap pieces RST. Match up all edges, pin and stitch all around the sides and bottom. Clip the curves, iron the seams open, turn the flap RSO and iron using a pressing cloth. Attach the seam allowance guide (if using) to your sewing machine and topstitch the flap all around the side and curvy bottom edges with a 1cm (⅜in) seam allowance.

18 **Apply the twist lock front plates** – follow steps 4–6 on page 93 to insert the twist lock plates to the RS of the bag flap at the twist lock markings.

Assembling the bag

19 **Stitch the flap to the bag exterior** – pin the flap WSU to the RS of the bag exterior. Place the flap onto the centre top edge of the bag exterior back. Match up the raw edges and stitch the flap to the exterior bag back with a 5mm (³⁄₁₆in) seam allowance. See **Fig g**.

Fig g *Pin the flap to the bag exterior and stitch it in place with a 5mm (³⁄₁₆in) seam allowance.*

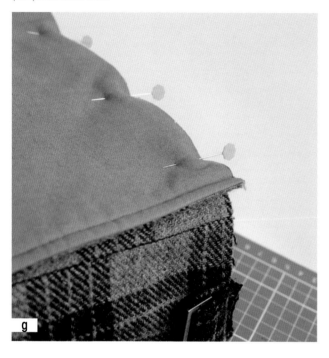

g

20 **Stitch the bag lining to the bag exterior** – insert the exterior bag RSO into the lining bag WSO. The right sides of the exterior bag and the lining bag should now be touching each other. Pin all around the top edge and stitch all around the top edge. See steps 4 and 5 of pull through and turn out lining method, page 75.

21 **Turn the bag RSO** – reach into the gap in the lining and pull the exterior bag out through the hole. Push the exterior bag into the lining. Stitch the gap in the lining shut by pushing the raw edges of the gap in the lining into the hole and topstitching shut. Smooth out any bumps and iron the bag using a pressing cloth (paying extra attention to neatening the top edge). See steps 5 and 6 of pull through and turn out lining method, page 75.

22 **Topstitch the top of the bag** – with the bag flap open topstitch all around the bag top edge with a 1cm (³⁄₈in) seam allowance.

23 **Attach the adjustable strap to the bag** – follow steps 2–3 on pages 106–107 to attach the adjustable strap.

Below *The days of carrying a seperate handbag, book bag and laptop bag are over – this office bag does it all in one organized package! Make it in a modern fabric such as this graphic print for a really stylish look.*

5: CLOSURES

Closures are an essential component to all but the simplest tote bags. Without a secure fastening on your bag you'd have the contents spilling out everywhere while running for the bus and you'd also be making life easy for 'naughty fingers'. But just because bag closures are functional doesn't mean they have to look boring. Experiment with positioning and choosing your fastening type and you'll end up with bag closures that look like eye-catching design features. A shiny metal clasp here and a slanted zipper there ... zhush up your bags with closures that are just as fun as they are functional.

The professionals ...
It's worth getting to grips with the different types of snaps and zips – a neatly inserted closure will give your bags a super-professional finish.

CLOSURE TYPE	BENEFITS	SUGGESTED USES
Top Edge Zip: pages 83 and 86	One of the easier zips to master, perfect for simple tote bags.	Cosmetics purses, tote bags and coin purses.
Concealed Top Edge Zip: pages 83 and 88	Gives the top of the bag a boxier look. As the zip is hidden, the top of the bag looks very neat.	Tote bags, document/laptop bags and shoulder bags.
Box Top Zip: pages 83 and 90	Adds space and a flat surface to the top edge of the bag. Great for boxier bags.	Overnight bags, sports-style round duffle bags, over-the-body satchels and hold-alls.
Magnetic Snap: pages 84 and 91	Quick and easy to apply, versatile, neat and inexpensive.	Many types of bags, pocket flaps, wallet and journal tab closures.
Invisible Magnetic Snap: pages 84 and 91	Snap has a flat profile and is concealed so gives a neat and flush appearance to the bag flap.	Many types of bags, pocket flaps, wallet and journal tab closures.
Twist Lock: pages 85 and 92	Highly decorative and provides fast access to your bag.	Messenger bag flaps, pocket flaps, bag tab closures, journal tab closures.
Eyelets and Rivets: page 85	Quick to apply. Great for using on lots of layers.	Attaching many types of handles and straps, and adding decorative features.

Zips

They may send shivers into many a new bag maker, but zips are so effective and useful that they are hard to avoid and besides, they are actually quite easy to use. There are three basic types of zip:

• conventional (also known as non-separating)
• separating
• invisible

Most bag makers tend to stick to the conventional variety – the other two types are more for dressmaking. Have fun choosing a zip to use on your bag and play with your colour choice. The zip colour doesn't always need to match the bag fabric. How about a zingy contrasting coloured zip?

Top Edge Zip These are very useful and quick and easy to apply. If you haven't used a zip in bag making before, attempt this type of zip first – you'll be delighted with the results and be really proud of yourself. See pages 86–87.

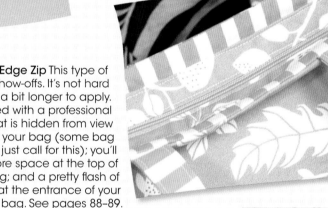

Concealed Top Edge Zip This type of zip is one for the show-offs. It's not hard to do, it just takes a bit longer to apply. You'll be rewarded with a professional looking closure that is hidden from view from the outside of your bag (some bag designs just call for this); you'll get more space at the top of your bag; and a pretty flash of colour at the entrance of your bag. See pages 88–89.

Put on weight …
Experiment with the weight choice of your zips, matching and contrasting them with your fabric weight – chunky can look funky!

Box Top Zip This is perfect for when you want the top of your bag to zip shut leaving the maximum amount of volume at the top. The top of your bag will have a flat profile and you can make the depth as deep as you want (without overdoing it proportion-wise, of course). See page 90.

NEED TO KNOW

❧ Zips are available in a rainbow of colours and in many different lengths, weights and materials, such as brass, nickel and nylon. The heavier the zip the more wear and tear it can stand.

❧ Conventional zips are closed at one end so that the zip pull can't be pulled off the zip.

Snaps and locks

Used singly or in pairs, snaps and locks are a fantastically versatile way to fasten your bags. Not only are they practical, but like any good accessory, they can dress a bag up or down. For example, magnetic fastenings look great on an urban messenger bag, and are quick to open and close. A twist lock adds a touch of old-school glamour to a posh handbag, and they have a satisfyingly 'grown-up' feel when you're using them.

Magnetic snaps A set of magnetic snaps comprises two metal washers and a male (non-magnetic) part, which is attracted to a female (magnetic) part. They are as easy to apply as making a cuppa; in fact they were my first foray into the world of shiny metal bag bits. They are simple, clean looking, versatile and inexpensive. Magnetic snaps are available in various sizes, colours and shapes, but round and rectangular are the most widely available. See page 91.

Opposites attract ...
Before stitching the snap half in position just quickly check that it will attract the other half and will not repel it instead.

Invisible snaps A set of invisible magnetic snaps comprises two parts, both of which are low-profile metal discs (which are attracted to each other) enclosed in a clear PVC pad. They may not look very exciting, but invisible snaps are so useful when you want a magnetic closure that is flat in profile and is hidden from view. Sometimes you don't want to see your magnetic snap because you want your purse or bag to work the minimalist look, or want your closure to be nice and flat (like you perhaps would on a dainty sized clutch or a journal cover). See page 91.

Pulling power ...
Magnetic snaps are available in different heights – standard and low profile (for a slimmer, lower fat look). The larger the magnet snap the stronger the pulling power.

Twist locks A screw-in type twist lock comprises a front plate, a twist button and a washer. Twist locks are available in a wide range of metal colours, shapes and sizes. Pop one of these fastenings on your bag for a super professional look. In terms of fun equals function I don't think you can beat a twist lock, they are an instant way for your handmade bags to move into the realms of handcrafted arm candy. If twist locks make crazy-price designer handbags look expensive, they'll work a treat on your handmade bags. See pages 92–93.

Living together ... If instructions come with the hardware, make sure you locate them and keep it all together so that they're handy for next time.

EYELETS AND RIVETS

Some hardware comes with its own instructions. You'll find all the parts required, plus the tools to apply them, in the pack.

Eyelets These are so versatile in bag making. Not only are they quick to apply, they can handle umpteen fabric layers and you can hook or thread all manner of things through the eyelets such as chain, bag straps, metalware or piped bag handles.

- In bag making, eyelets are as useful as they are decorative. Use eyelets to attach your bag straps, rings and snaps onto or use them for drawstring closures or even corset-style decorative lacing.
- Pick the perfect sized eyelet for the width of your bag strap, snap hook or lace etc. or try oversized eyelets for a cool, decorative design feature.
- Any eyelet kit will come with detailed instructions on how to apply the eyelets. Read the instructions carefully then dive in and have fun adding eyelets wherever you want them.

Rivets These are super useful in bag making, I love using them. Rivets are used to strongly join fabrics together and/or as a decorative trim.

- Use them whenever there are too many layers for your sewing machine, or when sewing is too awkward, or even when you are simply in a hurry!
- There are often times when your bag strap is too thick to be sewn to your (already) layer-tastic bag and this is where rivets can save the day. Not only are they effective, they look so professional!
- You'll need to invest in a hole punch and a rivet kit (where you'll find instructions on how to apply).
- They are simple to get the hang of and I'm sure that once you do you'll be riveting all over the place!

Top Edge Zip

This tutorial shows you how to insert a top edge zip into a pencil case, but the method would be the same for a tote bag, for example. Zips may look scary, but they are quite simple to apply. Start off with this top edge zip technique and you'll wonder why you stayed away from them for so long.

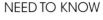

NEED TO KNOW

● All seam allowances are 1cm (⅜in) unless stated otherwise.

You will need

- Nylon all-purpose zip, 20cm (8in)
- 2 pieces of home dec exterior fabric, 24 x 10cm (9½ x 4in) for the exterior main body
- 2 pieces of home dec exterior fabric, 4 x 3.5cm (1½ x 1⅜in) for the zip tab
- 2 pieces of lining fabric 24 x 10cm (9½ x 4in) for the lining main body
- Zipper sewing machine foot
- Pins
- Pointy tool (such as a knitting needle)

a

Fig a *Fabric tabs on the zip will make the zip lie flat at the top corners of the case and also help to make it look pretty.*

1 **Trim the zip with the zip tabs** – take one of the zip tab fabric pieces RSU and fold under one of the short edges 1cm (⅜in). Place the folded edge of the zip tab onto the RS of one of the ends of the zip and stitch along the folded edge. See **Fig a**. The raw zip tab edge should meet the zip end edge. Repeat with the other zip tab and the other end of the zip.

2 **Attach one side of the zip onto one side of the pencil case** – make a zipper sandwich as follows. Starting from the bottom: lining fabric piece RSO on the bottom, zip RSO in the middle, and exterior piece WSO on the top. Carefully and neatly match up all of the edges and pin the layers at the long top edge. See **Fig b**. Attach the zipper foot to your sewing machine and stitch through the three layers, along the pencil case top edge. Stitch with a 5mm (³⁄₁₆in) seam allowance.

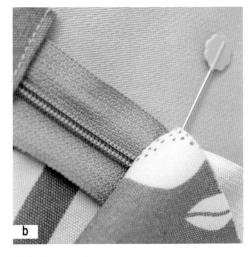

b

Fig b *Make up a three-layered zippy sandwich as shown.*

c1

c2

3 Topstitch the zip on the RS of the pencil case – flip the layers over so that the exterior and the zip is RSO. Topstitch neatly along the folded edge of the exterior fabric. Repeat steps 2 and 3 with the other side of the zip and the exterior and lining fabric pieces. See **Fig c**.

Fig c1–c2 *Topstitch along the folded edge – this should be the result: one zip inserted neatly into your lining and exterior fabrics.*

4 Pin and stitch the pencil case together – nb: ensure the zip is unzipped. Flip the fabric layers over so that the RS of the lining pieces are touching each other and the RS of the exterior pieces are touching each other. Match up the edges all around and pin – the zip will naturally curve towards the lining. See **Fig d1**. Stitch all around the pencil case, but leave a gap of 8cm (3⅛in) in the bottom edge of the lining. See **Fig d2**. Clip off all corners.

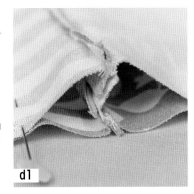

d1

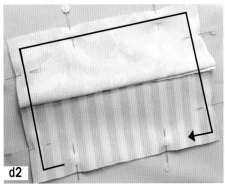

d2

Fig d1 *Pin the case as shown, the zip will naturally curve up towards the lining.*

Fig d2 *Following the drawn line, stitch along the sides and bottom of the case leaving a gap in the lining.*

Careful clipping ...
When clipping off all the corners, take extra care not to cut through your stitches.

5 Turn the pencil case right side out – reach into the gap in the lining and through the open zip to turn the pencil case RSO. See **Fig e**. So that's why the zip needed to be open! Push all the corners out using a pointy tool such as a fat knitting needle.

6 Stitch the gap in the lining shut – fold the raw edges of the gap 1cm (⅜in) into the hole, press and topstitch the hole shut. Smooth out any bumps and iron the case.

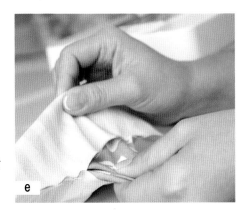

e

Fig e *Pull the exterior case out through the hole in the case lining.*

Concealed Top Edge Zip

This bag top zip closure looks very neat and professional because the zip is hidden from view.

NEED TO KNOW

- All seam allowances are 1cm (⅜in) unless stated otherwise.

- This style of zip is applied to the bag lining.

- Insert this type of zip closure BEFORE you assemble the bag lining. If you want to add any internal bag pockets to the lining you should add them BEFORE you insert the concealed top edge zip.

1 Trim the zip with the zip tab – bring the zip tab fabric pieces RST, pin and stitch together all around the sides and bottom, leaving a 4cm (1½in) gap for turning the zip tab RSO. Turn the zip tab RSO though the gap and iron. Take the closed zip end and fold the zip tab in half over the zip pull end (so as to encase the zip end). Match all edges of the zip tab, pin and topstitch all around the zip tab to the zip pull end. See **Fig a**.

2 Make up a casing for both sides of the zip – take one of the zip casing fabric pieces WSO and fold in both short edges 1cm (⅜in). Then fold in half lengthways, iron along the crease and open out. Finally fold in the long edges into the centre crease you have just made. See **Fig b**. Repeat with the other zip casing piece.

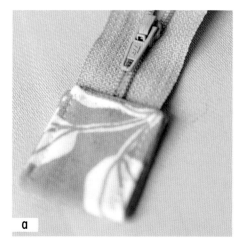

a

Fig a *The zip tab looks professional and it gives you something to grab hold of when opening and closing the zip.*

Fig b *Fold in both short edges 1cm (⅜in); fold the casing in half lengthways and open out; fold the long edges into the centre crease and fold in half so the casing resembles a book jacket cover.*

b

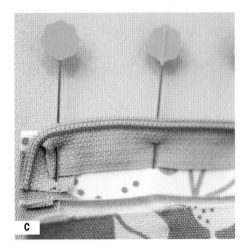

3 **Pin the zip into the zip casing** – first unzip the zip. With the zip RSU take the raw end of the zip (which has no zip tab attached) and fold and pin the zip fabric end to the casing (which is opened out). See **Fig c**. Pin the zip 3mm (⅛in) from the folded edge of the zip casing. Repeat with the other zip casing and zip half.

Fig c *The raw end of the zip is folded down so the zip stops just short of the short edge of the casing. Folding the fabric end of the zip down like this will neatly conceal the raw edge of the zip inside the finished casing.*

4 **Stitch the zip half into the casing** – attach the zipper foot to your sewing machine and turn the casing RSO (still opened out and with the zip pinned on). Topstitch the zip into position in the casing along the long edge. Turn over the casing and fold it closed. Topstitch all around the open edges of the casing to trap the zip inside. See **Fig d**.

Perfect symmetry ...
Take care to position the second zip casing half as symmetrically as you can or the zip won't look good, or work well.

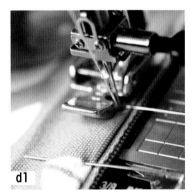

d1 **d2** **d3**

Fig d1–d3 *Topstitching the zip into position; topstitching around the casing; the result.*

5 **Attach the zip to your bag lining** – unzip the zip and, working with one half of the zip at a time, measure and mark the centre of your zip and also the centre top edge of your bag lining piece. Decide how far down you would like your concealed zip to sit inside your bag – a good guide is 3cm (1⅛in) down from the finished top edge. So, after adding on a top edge seam allowance of 5mm (³⁄₁₆in), position the concealed zip 3.5cm (1⅜in) down from the top edge of the bag lining fabric. Pin and topstitch the zip casing RSO to the RS of the lining along the top edge. See **Fig e**. Repeat with the other casing half and bag lining piece. And there you have one concealed top edge zip inserted into you lining pieces. You can now complete the construction of your lining and the rest of your bag (see page 156).

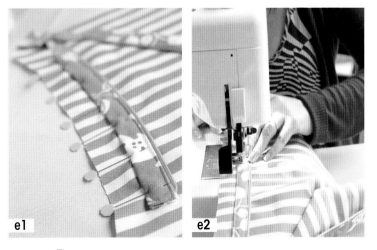

e1 **e2**

Fig e1–e2 *The zip casing is pinned into position to your bag lining.*

Box Top Zip

This zip closure is one for the show-offs! It looks really professional, adds another splash of colour and it adds loads of room to the top and sides of your bag.

You will need

- Nylon all-purpose zip
- 2 rectangles of exterior fabric for the zip top/side panels
- 2 rectangles of lining fabric for the zip top/side panels
- 2 rectangles of exterior fabric for the zip bottom panels
- 2 rectangles of exterior fabric for the zip tabs
- Zipper sewing machine foot

NEED TO KNOW

- This zip is inserted into the top and side panels of your bag. Therefore, this zip is only suitable for boxy shaped bags.
- Choose a zip that is the same length as the desired zip opening length, such as 80cm (31½in).
- The bag you are making will dictate the dimensions of the fabrics needed to make this style of zip. For this reason you will find the full instructions as part of The Great Getaway Bag on pages 112–121. Have a go at inserting a box top zip into that project first and you'll then be able to insert one into your own design bags.
- When using a box top zip, add any internal pockets BEFORE you assemble the lining.

General advice

- A box top zip is formed of nine parts: a zipper, two long exterior fabric panels for the top and side edges, two long lining fabric panels for the top and side edges, two exterior bottom panels, and two lining bottom panels.
- When the above parts are all stitched together the length of the box top zip should equal the combined length of both sides and the top edge of the bag.
- The two long exterior fabric top/side panels are machine stitched either side of the long edges of the zip and then bottom panels are stitched to the short ends of the zip (with top/side panels attached). The exterior zip is then ready to be attached to your bag exterior. See **Fig a**.
- For the box top zip lining, the bag lining is fully constructed with all zip panels stitched together, minus the zip, which leaves a long, thin rectangular hole along the top and sides of the bag lining to which the zip will be stitched. See **Fig b**.
- The bag lining is then stitched to the bag exterior along the bag bottom edge seams and finally the edges of the long thin hole in the lining are hand stitched to the fabric of the zip.

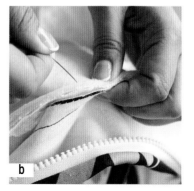

Fig a *The zip bottom panel and the zip top panel are stitched RST, then the zip bottom panel is folded down and topstitched along the top fold.*

Fig b *The bag lining is made up in the same way as for the bag exterior except there are no zip or zip parts to insert. You will be left with a lining bag that has a long, thin rectangular hole along the top.*

Snaps

A magnetic snap closure is so speedy and easy to apply. However, if you think that a visible closure would spoil the look of your bag, try using an invisible magnetic snap instead.

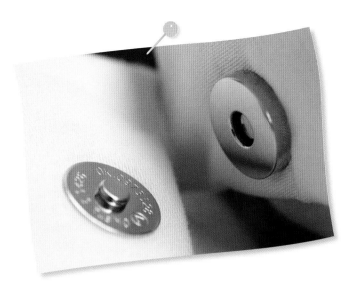

You will need

Magnetic snap

- Magnetic snap
- 2 squares of fusible interfacing for magnetic snap reinforcement, 2.5cm (1in)
- Seam ripper

Invisible magnetic snap

- Invisible magnetic snap
- Zipper sewing machine foot

NEED TO KNOW

- Even if your fabric is heavy, it's essential to reinforce the magnetic snap area of the fabric. This is because the fabric will be put under repeated strain by the pulling of the magnet.

- Invisible magnetic snaps are usually sewn to the interlining or onto the WS of the bag lining.

- If your bag is made from a few fabric and interfacing layers, or your fabrics are on the heavy side, cut a small, round magnet-sized hole though your interlining layers (if using). This exposes the magnet so it doesn't loose its strength through all of the layers.

- Insert snaps BEFORE assembling your bag lining, bag exterior or bag flap.

MAGNETIC SNAP

1 **Reinforce the magnetic snap fabric area** – iron an interfacing square to the WS of the fabric where you have chosen to insert your magnetic snap. Repeat with the other interfacing square and the other fabric piece. If you are applying your snap to the exterior (for example, for bag or pocket flaps) of your bag and you are using interlining, at this point you need to lay your exterior RSO onto your interlining piece and treat them both as one layer.

2 **Make incisions for the snap and apply** – using a seam ripper, make two tiny incisions through all of the fabric layers for the magnetic snap prongs. Take one half of the magnetic snap and push the prongs through the incisions through RS of the bag fabric. Place a metal washer over the prongs at the back of the bag fabric and push the prongs down firmly away from each other. See **Fig a**. Repeat with the other magnetic snap half.

INVISIBLE MAGNETIC SNAP

1 **Prepare the magnetic snap area** – if using interlining (as described in the box above) cut a small hole though your interlining to expose the magnet. See **Fig b**. If you are not using interlining proceed to step 2.

2 **Stitch the invisible snap to your bag fabric** – attach the zipper foot to your sewing machine and stitch one half of the invisible snap to the magnetic snap marking on the fabric. Sew in a box formation around the magnet. Repeat with the other snap half.

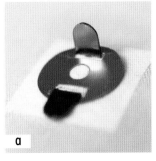

a

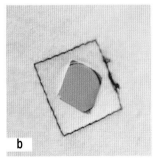

b

Fig a *View of magnetic snap half from the WS of the bag. Push the prongs down firmly.*

Fig b *Exposing the magnet by cutting through the layers will help the magnet retain its pulling power.*

Twist Lock

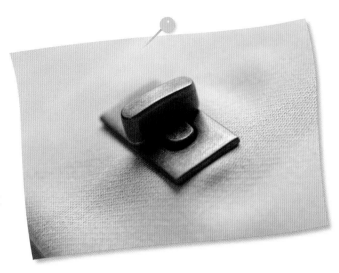

There's nothing like a bit of shiny metal on a bag to make you think 'ohh pretty'! Twist locks not only look lovely but they are also useful. Pop a twist lock on your bag to instantly elevate it from 'homemade' to 'handcrafted'. It works every time …

You will need

- Twist lock (sometimes known as a turn lock)
- 2 squares of fusible interfacing for reinforcement, 2.5cm (1in).
- Seam ripper
- Small sharp scissors
- Small screwdriver
- Disappearing marker

NEED TO KNOW

⊛ Even if your fabric is heavy, it's essential to reinforce the twist lock area of the fabric, as it will be put under repeated strain by the weight and the pulling of the twist lock.

⊛ Twist locks work best on bags made from heavier fabrics or several layers. This is because these metal locks can be heavy and your bag needs to be able to support the weight without sagging.

⊛ The twist button part of the lock is applied to the bag exterior BEFORE you assemble the exterior bag. The front plate part of the lock is inserted at the very end, AFTER you have assembled your bag.

1 Reinforce the twist lock fabric area – iron an interfacing square to the WS of the fabric where you have chosen to insert your twist lock. If you are applying your twist lock to the exterior of your bag and you are using interlining, at this point you need to lay your exterior RSO onto your interlining piece and treat them both as one layer.

Fig a1–a3 Make two tiny holes for the prongs; slip the washer over the prongs at the back; the result – one nice, straight twist button.

2 Apply the button part of the twist lock to the bag exterior front of your bag – using a seam ripper, make two tiny incisions through all layers (your exterior fabric and your interlining) for the prongs of the button part of the lock. Ensure the lock is sitting nice and straight at the front on your bag. Push the prongs of the button part of the lock through the incisions on the RS of the bag fabric. Slip a metal washer over the prongs at the back of the bag fabric and push the prongs down firmly towards each other so that the lock is secured into position. See **Fig a**.

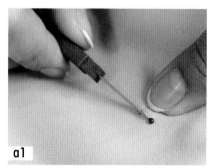

a1

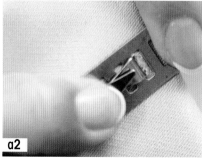

a2

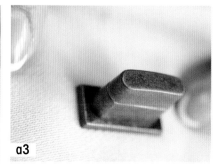

a3

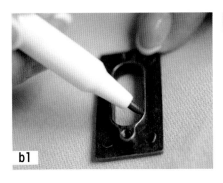

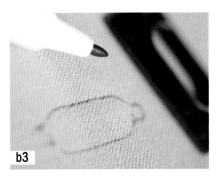

b1   b2   b3

3 **Finish making your bag flap and your bag** – make up your bag flap. As you are doing this don't forget to reinforce the twist lock area of your bag flap (as in step 1). Finish making up your bag before applying the twist front plate to the bag.

4 **Mark the front plate position onto your bag flap** – with your bag assembled; pull your bag flap down over the twist button part of the lock (as if you are closing the flap on your bag). Mark the point on the bag flap where the flap falls directly onto the twist button. Unscrew the screws on the front plate and you'll see that one half of the twist plate has a raised lip (top). Use a disappearing marker to draw onto the raised lip (including the outer side of the screw holes). Press the inky twist plate onto the RS of the bag flap at the marking you made earlier. The ink imprint that gets left behind will serve as a cutting guide for the next step. See **Fig b**.

Fig b1–b3 Mark the front plate position on your flap; ink the raised lip of the opened up front plate; press the front plate down to leave an ink imprint for use as a cutting guide.

Call for reinforcements ...
You can use whatever weight of interfacing you have to hand. If you think that your interfacing is too lightweight try fusing a couple of interfacing squares on top of each other.

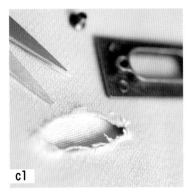

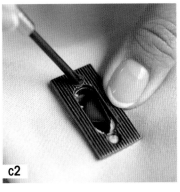

c1   c2

Fig c1–c2 View of the front plate from the lining side of the bag; here's the result viewed from the back. Screwing one of the screws into the lock will make it much easier to remove any straggly bits of fabric from the hole in the lock.

One snip at a time ...
The hole you cut must be slightly too small or the twist plate will not be held in tightly by the fabric, making it unsecure.

5 **Cut a hole for the front plate** – using the cutting guide that you made in the previous step, use small sharp scissors to cut a hole that is slightly smaller than the ink imprint. When cutting the hole take your time, cut a bit and then test the plate, then cut a bit and test and so on.

6 **Assemble the front plate onto your bag flap** – sandwich the bag flap in between the front and back halves of the front plate at the hole you made in the previous step. The shiny front part of the front plate is positioned onto the RS of the bag flap, and the back part of the plate goes on the back of the flap. Screw in the screws of the front plate at the back of the bag flap, at the same time ensure that the front plate hole is kept free of any stray bits of fabric. You might need to stretch and tug the fabric around the hole a little to accommodate the front plate. See **Fig c**.

Make it...
The Oversized Fashionista Bag

This roomy bag is a cute and quirky take on the classic clutch bag. The bag's chi-chi metal accessories and closures look oh-so expensive while being totally functional. The metal twist lock closure and the eyelets add both style and substance to the design. There's even a zip inside the bag too. The girls just aren't going to believe that you whipped up this gorgeous bag yourself!

Side view *The bag darts add a soft 3D silhouette and a little volume to the bag.*

Shoulder strap *The removable metal chain strap makes an interesting feature.*

Lining pocket *A flush zip pocket ensures all of your smaller-sized essentials are secure and easy to access.*

NEED TO KNOW

- A heavier fabric is best for the exterior of this bag because of the bag's size. Fabric suggestions include velvet, heavy wools, real or faux leather or suede, cotton, canvas or denim.

- If using leather, only pin in the seam allowance so as not to 'scar' the material with pinholes. For more advice on working with leather see page 33.

- Be sure to use a jeans sewing machine needle if using heavy fabrics.

- All seam allowances are 1cm (⅜in) unless stated otherwise.

- Pattern pieces are given in the pull-out section and include the 1cm (⅜in) seam allowance.

You will need

- I piece of home dec fabric for exterior, 1m (1yd) x 1.5m (1½yd) wide
- 1 piece of fabric for lining, 1m (1yd) x 1.5m (1½yd) wide
- 1 piece of medium or firm fusible interfacing, 1m (1yd)
- 2 pieces of fusible fleece, 1m (1yd)
- Nylon zip, 18cm (7in)
- Flexi-tube, 39cm (15⅜in)
- Heavy purse chain, 28cm (11in)
- 2 metal eyelets, 14mm (½in)
- 4 bolt snaps, 2.5cm (1in)
- 2 D-rings, 12mm (½in)
- Twist lock
- Zipper sewing machine foot

Preparation

Cut the fabric and interfacing pieces as follows:

From Fashionista (main body) pattern piece (see pull-out section)
- 2 x exterior fabric
- 2 x fusible interfacing
- 2 x lining fabric
- 2 x fusible fleece

From Fashionista (flap) pattern piece (see pull-out section)
- 1 x exterior fabric
- 1 x fusible interfacing
- 1 x lining fabric
- 1 x fusible fleece

Transfer all pattern notches and markings to the fabric with a disappearing marker.

Also cut:

- 2 pieces of lining fabric, 28 x 20cm (11 x 8in), for the flush zip pocket
- 2 pieces of exterior fabric, 6 x 11cm (2⅜ x 4⅜in), for the shoulder strap loops
- 1 piece of exterior fabric, 56 x 18cm (22 x 7in), for the shoulder strap
- 1 piece of exterior fabric, 10 x 5cm (4 x 2in), for the shoulder strap chain loops
- 1 piece of exterior fabric, 50 x 15cm (19½ x 6in), for the piped handle
- 2 pieces of fusible interfacing, 5cm (2in) square, for the twist lock reinforcement

The interfacing, strap and handle

1 Interface the exterior fabric pieces – match the fusible interfacing pattern pieces to their partner fabric pattern pieces and iron them to the WS of the fabric pieces. Iron the twist lock reinforcement interfacing squares to the WS of the bag exterior front and the bag exterior flap pieces, behind the markings for the twist lock. Finally, iron the fusible fleece pattern pieces onto the WS of all of the exterior fabric pieces (directly onto the fusible interfacing).

2 **Make the shoulder strap** – three different parts that are combined to make the strap as follows:
- Shoulder strap chain loops: take the shoulder strap chain loop fabric piece and follow the steps on page 102 to make one open-end strap. Divide the resulting strap into two equal lengths and thread a small D-ring onto each of the chain loop straps.
- Shoulder strap: take the shoulder strap fabric piece and follow the steps on page 103 to make one closed-end strap. Before you topstitch all around the closed strap, place a shoulder strap chain loop (folded in half with D-ring still attached) at either end of the shoulder strap. Fold the strap shut and stitch all around the shoulder strap trapping the chain loops inside as you sew. Divide the purse chain into two equal lengths. Use pliers to open the end links and attach the chain to the D-rings on the shoulder strap. See **Fig a**. Set the shoulder strap aside.
- Shoulder strap loops: take the shoulder strap loop pieces and follow the steps on page 103 to make two closed-end straps. Thread the bolt snaps onto the shoulder strap loops and set aside.

a1

a2

Fig a1–a2 *Place folded chain loops at both short edges of the shoulder strap, stitch the strap shut, attach the chain and this will be the result.*

b

3 **For the piped handle** – take the piped handle fabric piece and follow the steps on page 103 to make one closed-end strap. Now follow the steps on pages 108–109 to make one piped handle. Thread a bolt snap onto either end of the piped handle. Fold the fabric end of the handle over the bolt snap ring and securely stitch the fabric end down. See **Fig b**. Set the piped handle aside.

Fig b *Stitch the fabric end down over the ring of the bolt snap.*

The bag exterior

4 **Insert the twist lock button** – follow step 2 on page 92 to insert the twist lock button to the bag exterior front at the twist lock marking.

5 **Sew the darts on the exterior pieces** – fold the V-shape of the dart in half RST and stitch along the raw edges with a 5mm (³⁄₁₆in) seam allowance, following step 2 on page 49. Repeat with the other three darts.

6 **Part stitch the exterior pieces together and attach the shoulder strap loops** – because this bag is made from several layers it's easier to stitch shoulder strap loops to the outside of the bag. Part stitching the exterior pieces together makes it easier to stitch the shoulder strap loops on, as it will prevent you from getting into a tangle with the sewing machine. Pin and stitch the bag exterior pieces RST at the side seams only, 13cm (5⅛in) down from the top edge. Now turn the exterior bag RSO and press the side seams open. Take one of the shoulder strap loops (with bolt snap still attached) and position the loop at the pattern marking. Hold it in place with your finger and stitch to the side seam in a box formation (for strength). See **Fig c**. Repeat with the other shoulder strap loop. Turn the bag exterior WSO.

7 **Finish stitching the exterior pieces together** – pin the rest of the bag exterior pieces RST. When matching up the exterior pieces take care to match up the dart lines on both of the fabric pieces. See **Fig d** and step 3 on page 49. Sew all around the sides and the bottom edge of the exterior. Clip the curves, being careful not to cut the seams (see page 19). Turn RSO.

Fig d *For professional-looking bag darts match up the dart lines at the front and back.*

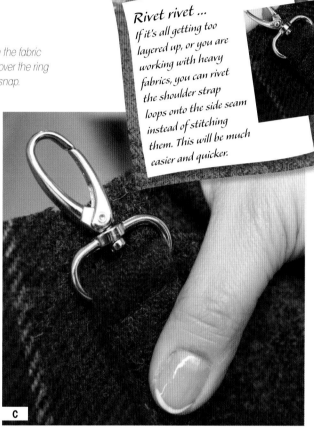

Rivet rivet ...
If it's all getting too layered up, or you are working with heavy fabrics, you can rivet the shoulder strap loops onto the side seam instead of stitching them. This will be much easier and quicker.

c

Fig c *The strap loop and bolt snap need to face up towards the top edge of the bag.*

d

The bag lining

8 Insert a flush zip pocket into the lining – take the zip and the flush zip pocket fabric pieces and follow the steps on pages 66–69 to insert a flush zip pocket. Insert the pocket into one of the bag lining pieces using the pocket pattern markings as a guide.

9 Sew the darts on the lining and stitch the lining together – sew both darts and assemble the lining as in steps 5 and 7 on page 97, but leave a gap of 18cm (7in) in the bottom edge of the lining for turning out.

The bag flap

10 Stitch the bag flap – bring the bag exterior and lining bag flap pieces RST. Match up all edges, pin and stitch all around the sides and bottom. Clip the curves and snip the corners. Turn the bag flap RSO and iron. Topstitch all around the side and curvy bottom edge with a 1cm (⅜in) seam allowance.

11 Apply the twist lock front plate – following steps 4–6 on page 93. See **Fig e**.

e

Fig e *One slick-looking bag flap with twist lock plate attached.*

Above *You can get totally different looks by having fun with your fabric choices for this bag. How about trying a summer shabby chic look from using quilted pastel coloured patchwork, faded denim with a some cute appliqué work, or linen/velvet fabric trimmed with a contrast fat piped edge (see pages 144 –145)? And check out the hot pink wool I've used here – definitely not your average tweed!*

Assembling the bag

12 **Stitch the bag flap to the bag exterior** – pin the flap WSU to the RS of the bag exterior. Place the flap onto the centre top edge of the bag exterior back. Match up the raw edges and stitch the flap to the exterior bag back with a 5mm (³⁄₁₆in) seam allowance. See **Fig f**.

13 **Stitch the lining bag to the exterior bag** – insert the exterior bag RSO into the lining bag WSO. The right sides of the exterior bag and the lining bag should now be touching each other. See **Fig g1**. Match up the raw top edges and side seams for neatness, pin at the top edge and stitch all around the top.

14 **Turn the bag right side out** – reach into the gap in the lining and pull the exterior bag out through the hole. See **Fig g2**. Push the exterior bag into the lining. Stitch the gap in the lining shut by pushing the raw edges of the gap in the lining into the hole and topstitching shut. Smooth out any bumps and iron the bag (paying extra attention to neatening the top edge).

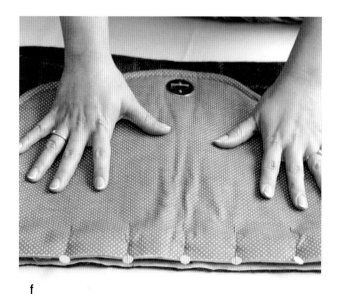

f

Fig f *Pin the bag flap to the bag exterior and stitch it in place with a 5mm (³⁄₁₆in) seam allowance.*

g1

Fig g1 *Place the exterior bag completely into the lining bag.*

g2

Fig g2 *Gently pull the exterior bag through the hole you left in the lining.*

15 **Apply eyelets to the bag flap** – fold the bag down at the bag flap crease pattern markings. Ensuring the flap is central and straight, iron the top edge of the flap. Stitch a line though the folded flap 3cm (1⅛in) down from the folded top edge. Follow the eyelet kit instructions to apply the eyelets to the bag flap eyelet pattern markings (in between the top edge and the line of stitching you have just sewn). Clip the piped handle onto the eyelets.

16 **Finishing touches** – with the flap open, topstitch the bag top edge with a 1cm (⅜in) seam allowance and clip the shoulder strap onto the shoulder strap loops.

Take your time ...
When stitching the lining bag to the exterior bag, it will be a little bulky, particularly at the bag of the bag where the flap is situated. Just take it slowly to get a neat result.

6: HANDLES AND STRAPS

Bag handles are so much more than mere straps to keep your bags off the floor. Whether you are plumping for fabric, rope, metal, acrylic, wood or leather handles, they can be exciting design features in their own right. Experiment with colour and texture – add some expensive-looking chain or 'upcycle' a vintage scarf into some swish handles that will carry off your bag in style. This chapter looks at various types of handmade handles and how to attach them to your creations. The table below shows the more commonly used handmade bag handles and their best uses.

Window shopping ... I've also shown you some of the ready-made handles available to buy if time is short.

HANDLE TYPE	BENEFITS	SUGGESTED USES
Open-Ended Straps: page 102	Versatile, basic and strong, One of the easiest to make. These straps require no extra accessories.	Any type of bag. Make smaller versions for use as handle loops – needed for attaching various types of handles to your bags.
Closed-End Straps: page 103	As above.	Any type of bag. Also forms the basis of adjustable straps and piped handles (see below).
Two-Faced Straps: page 104	A decorative and more professional-looking fabric strap as the two fabrics echo the exterior and lining fabrics.	Any type of bag, but looks best where the bag is large enough to take a wider handle (to make the most of the handle's decorative looks).
Hook and Ring Straps: page 105	Detachable and the metalware makes these straps look very professional.	Any type of bag. Make smaller versions for use as a detachable wrist strap on wristlet clutches or even smaller versions for key loops to place in bag linings.
Adjustable Straps: page 106	Adjustable in length and professional looking.	Larger sized bags and/or bags worn across the body such as messenger/satchel/travel/hobo-style bags.
Piped Handles: page 108	'Designer' looks. Strong, upright, and comfortable to use.	Mid-to larger sized handbags such as daytime fashion bags and heavier hardworking bags such as weekender/travel and hold-all bags.

Open-End Straps These straps are simple, quick and effective. Because they are four layers thick they are strong. These straps are sewn in between your lining and exterior. You can also use this style of strap to make handle loops for attaching bag handles to your bags, as shown here. See page 102.

Closed-End Straps These straps are made in similar way to open-end straps, but because the ends are closed you stitch these handles onto the front of your bag or you can add metalware to the strap ends. See page 103.

Two-Faced Strap Made from two different fabrics (usually the lining and the exterior fabric), these straps are more decorative than the two previous straps. See page 104.

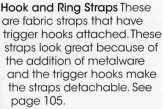

Hook and Ring Straps These are fabric straps that have trigger hooks attached. These straps look great because of the addition of metalware and the trigger hooks make the straps detachable. See page 105.

Adjustable Straps These straps might look confusing to make, but they are actually very easy and they are really satisfying to use and to look at. See pages 106–107.

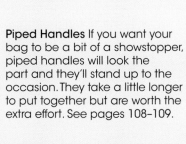

Piped Handles If you want your bag to be a bit of a showstopper, piped handles will look the part and they'll stand up to the occasion. They take a little longer to put together but are worth the extra effort. See pages 108–109.

Open-End Straps

These straps are quick and easy to make and are strong. Make smaller and shorter versions of this type of strap for handle loops – used for attaching certain types of bag handles to your bags. You can add metal rings to handle loops if desired. Open-end straps/handle loops are sewn in between the bag lining and exterior.

You will need

- Your choice of fabric in your chosen length (plus two lots of your chosen seam allowance). See Need To Know for how to gauge the width of your strap fabric
- The appropriate interfacing or padding for your choice of fabric (see page 31)
- Fusible fleece (optional). See Need To Know for how to gauge the width of your strap fleece

NEED TO KNOW

- To gauge the width of your strap fabric, first decide how wide you want your finished strap to be. Take that measurement and multiply it by four. If you want your finished strap to be 4cm (1½in) wide, your strap fabric needs to be 16cm (6¼in) wide.
- For comfort, add a little fusible fleece padding to the inside of your straps. To gauge the width of the fleece take the finished width measurement of your strap and divide it by two. If your finished strap is 4cm (1½in) wide, your fleece needs to be 2cm (¾in) wide.
- All seam allowances are 5mm (³⁄₁₆in) unless stated otherwise.
- Make up the bag lining, the exterior and the open-end straps/handle loops. Then stitch the handles in place to the RS of the exterior BEFORE you stitch the lining and the exterior together.

1 **Prepare your bag strap fabric** – ensure the strap fabric has been ironed, then iron the fusible interfacing (if using) to the WS of the bag strap fabric. Then iron the fleece strip (if using) to the centre WS of the bag strap.

2 **Fold and iron your strap** – with your strap fabric WSU fold the strap so that it resembles a book jacket cover as follows. With the strap fabric WSU fold the fabric in half lengthways and iron the centre crease. Open out and fold the long edges of the fabric to the centre crease and iron. Fold the whole strap in half lengthways again. See **Fig a**.

3 **Stitch the strap** – take the folded strap, give it an iron and pin along the long open edge. Topstitch along both long edges of the strap. The strap is now complete and ready to sew onto your bag (see Need To Know).

a

Fig a *Fold the strip of fabric so that the folds look like a book jacket cover.*

Closed-End Straps

As with open-end straps, these are quick and easy to make and are strong. Make these straps when you want to make adjustable straps (page 106) or you want to attach the ends of your bag straps onto the exterior side of your bag, or if you want to add metal rings or trigger hooks to the strap ends.

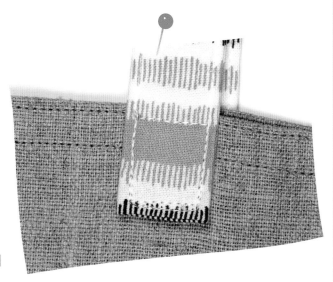

You will need

- Your choice of fabric in your chosen length plus two lots of your chosen seam allowance. See Need To Know for how to gauge the width of your strap fabric

- The appropriate interfacing or padding for your choice of fabric (see page 31)

- Fusible fleece (optional). See Need To Know for how to gauge the width of your strap fleece

NEED TO KNOW

⊕ To gauge the width of your strap fabric, first decide how wide you want your finished strap to be. Take that measurement and multiply it by four. If you want your finished strap to be 4cm (1½in) wide, your strap fabric needs to be 16cm (6¼in) wide.

⊕ For comfort, add a little fusible fleece padding to the inside of your straps. To gauge the width of the fleece take the finished width measurement of your strap and divide it by two. If your finished strap is 4cm (1½in) wide, your fleece needs to be 2cm (¾in) wide.

⊕ All seam allowances are 5mm (³/₁₆in) unless stated otherwise.

⊕ Closed-end straps are usually applied to bag at the VERY END of bag construction. If you want to add this style of strap to the front of your bag, finish making up your bag and stitch the strap ends to the RS exterior of your bag through all of the layers for strength.

1 Prepare your bag strap fabric – ensure the strap fabric has been ironed then iron the fusible interfacing (if using) to the WS of the strap fabric. Then iron the fleece strip (if using) to the centre WS of the strap.

2 Fold and iron your strap – with your strap fabric WSU fold both short edges in 1cm (⅜in) and iron the crease. Now fold the strap so that it resembles a book jacket cover as follows. With the strap fabric WSU fold the fabric in half lengthways and iron the centre crease. Open out and fold the long edges of the fabric to the centre crease and iron. Fold the whole strap in half lengthways again. See **Fig a**.

3 Stitch the strap – take the folded strap, give it an iron and pin along the long open edge. Topstitch all around the strap. The strap is now complete and ready to sew onto your bag (see Need To Know).

a

Fig a *Fold in the short edges of the strap before folding the strip of fabric so that folds look like a book jacket cover.*

Two-Faced Straps

Quick and easy to make, these straps are more decorative than the previous straps because they use two different fabrics (usually the lining fabric and the exterior fabric).

You will need

- Two different fabrics (ideally identical in weight) in your chosen length (plus two lots of your chosen seam allowance) x your chosen width (plus two lots of seam allowance)

- The appropriate interfacing or padding for your choice of fabric (see page 31)

- Fusible fleece (optional, for comfort) in your chosen strap length (plus two lots of seam allowance) x your chosen width (plus two lots of seam allowance)

- A large safety pin or a loop turner tool

NEED TO KNOW

- All seam allowances are 5mm (³/₁₆in) unless stated otherwise.

- When attaching this style strap to your bag treat it like an open-end strap (see page 102) by sewing it in between the bag lining and the exterior. Make up the lining, the exterior and the two-faced strap. Then stitch the straps in place to the RS of the exterior BEFORE you stitch the lining and the exterior together (see step 3, page 74).

1 **Prepare the strap fabric** – ensure the strap fabric has been ironed then iron the fusible interfacing (if using) to the WS of the strap fabric. Then iron the fleece strip (if using) to the centre WS of one of the strap fabric pieces.

2 **Stitch the strap** – bring your strap fabrics RST, pin and stitch along the both long edges to form a fabric tube. Iron the seams open on both long edges.

3 **Turn the strap RSO** – use a loop turner or pin a safety pin to one of the short edges of the fabric tube. Roll the raw edge of the fabric tube in on itself and begin pulling the safety pin up inside the tube so that the tube begins to turn itself RSO. See **Fig a**. Continue until the tube is fully RSO and remove the loop turner/safety pin.

4 **Stitch the strap** – iron the strap and topstitch along both long edges. The strap is now complete and ready to sew onto your bag (see Need To Know).

Iron with care ...
Before topstitching the finished strap, be precise when ironing the strap. You don't want any of the underside fabric to overhang and show on the right side of the strap.

Fig a *Hook the end of the loop turner/safety pin close to the edge of one of the short edges and pull the loop turner/safety pin up inside the tube.*

a

Hook and Ring Straps

A bit of metalware on your bag is a near instant way of lifting it from homemade to handmade. One of the easiest places to start experimenting with metalware on your bag is the handles.

You will need

- A finished closed-end strap (see page 103). To gauge the length of the closed-end strap see Need To Know
- 2 trigger hooks as wide as your finished strap
- 2 D-rings as wide as your finished strap
- 2–4 rivets and hole punch (optional)

NEED TO KNOW

⊕ To gauge the length of your strap decide how long you want the maximum length of your strap to be then add 10cm (4in). If you want your strap to be 80cm (31½in) long, your closed-end strap needs to be 90cm (35½in) long.

⊕ If your finished strap is thick you can rivet the hook into the strap. If your strap is up 2cm (¾in) wide, one rivet should be sufficient, but if your strap is wider then use two rivets (see page 85).

⊕ All seam allowances are 5mm (³∕₁₆in) unless stated otherwise.

⊕ Treat hook and ring straps in the same way as closed-end straps and apply them to your bag at the VERY END of bag construction. Usually you will have made handle loops (see page 102) with rings attached so you can clip the hook handles onto the rings. Finish making up your bag and simply clip the hook onto the rings of the handle loop.

1 **Stitch the hooks to the strap ends** – take your strap WSU and thread one end of the strap through the D-shaped ring of one of the trigger hooks. Fold the end over the D-ring by 2.5cm (1in) hold in position with your fingers and stitch the fabric end in place with a 3mm (¹∕₈in) seam allowance. Repeat with the other end of the strap and trigger hook.

2 **Alternatively, rivet the hooks to the strap** – take your strap WSU, fold one of the ends over by 2.5cm (1in) and punch a hole for the rivet(s) 5mm (³∕₁₆in) down from the edge of the strap through both layers. If the strap material is too thick to punch two layers at once, punch the hole through one at a time (fold the strap to mark the position of two punch holes). See **Fig a**. Thread the end of the strap through the D-ring of the trigger hook and rivet in place following the pack instructions.

Strapping suggestion ...
You can use leather straps and webbing as an alternative to fabric straps.

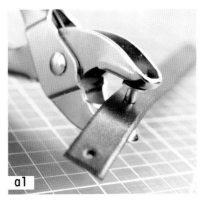

a1

a2

Fig a1–a2 *If the leather strap is quite narrow you can just use one rivet.*

Adjustable Straps

There is something really satisfying about making and using adjustable straps. Not only are they super practical they also look very swish.

You will need

- A finished closed-end strap (see page 103). To gauge the length of the closed-end strap see Need To Know

- 2 D-rings, as wide as your finished strap, each with its own handle loop (made from open-end straps, see page 102)

- 1 strap slider that is as wide as your finished strap

NEED TO KNOW

To gauge the length of your adjustable strap decide how long you want the maximum length of your strap to be, then add 10cm (4in). If you want the maximum length to be 1m (39in), your closed-end strap needs to be 110cm (43in) long.

All seam allowances are 5mm (³/₁₆in) unless stated otherwise.

An adjustable strap is attached to your bag at the END of bag making. In order to attach an adjustable strap to you bag you will need to attach handle loops (see page 102) with a D-ring attached.

1 Attach the handle loops – attach the handle loops (with D-rings attached) to the side seam of your bag (as in step 10 on page 79) and complete the construction of your bag (see page 156).

2 Stitch the metal slider to the strap – take your strap WSU and thread one end of the strap through the centre bar of the slider. Pull the strap end so it is free from the slider, pin and stitch the fabric end down. See **Fig a**.

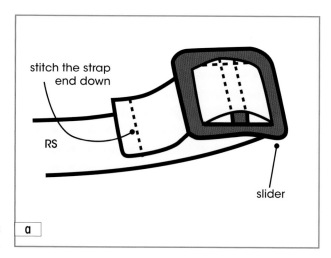

stitch the strap end down

RS

slider

a

Fig a *Pull the strap end through the slider so there is enough clearance for you to stitch the end down.*

3 Continue threading the strap – take the free end of the strap and thread it through the D-ring of one of the handle loops. Thread the strap end back through the slider and then thread it through the other D-ring of the other handle loop. Stitch the end down ensuring the strap end is folded onto the WS of your strap. See **Fig b**. Your adjustable strap is now strapped in and good to go!

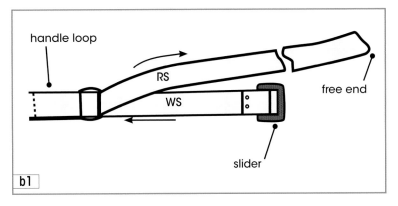

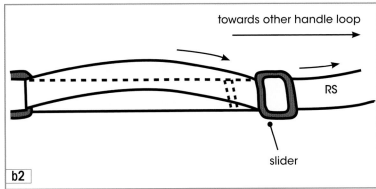

Fig b1–b2 Thread the strap through one of the D-rings and then back through the slider. Finally fold the end of the strap under the other D-ring and stitch the end down.

Below *An adjustable strap in action on this very smart looking office bag. Turn to pages 76–81 to make your own.*

Piped Handles

Of all the handmade bag handles, I think piped handles look the most 'posh' and professional. As they are very strong and comfortable to hold, they have substance as well as style.

You will need

- A finished closed-end strap (see page 103). To gauge the length and width of the closed-end strap see Need To Know
- A length of flexi-tube for stuffing the handles. To gauge the length of the tubing see Need To Know
- 2 trigger hooks as wide as your finished strap
- Disappearing marker

NEED TO KNOW

● To gauge the length of the finished closed-end strap, decide how long you want the length of your piped handle to be, then add 4cm (1½in). If you want the length of your piped handle to be 50cm (19½in) long, your closed end strap needs to be 54cm (21¼in) long.

● To gauge the finished width of the closed-end strap, measure around the circumference of your tubing and add 1cm (⅜in). If your tubing is 4cm (1½in) around, your closed-end strap needs to be 5cm (2in) wide.

● To gauge the length of the tubing measure the length of the closed-end strap and subtract 10cm (4in). If your closed-end strap is 54cm (21¼in) long, the tubing needs to be 44cm (17⅜in) long.

● All seam allowances are 1cm (⅜in) unless stated otherwise.

● Piped handles are attached to your bag at the END of bag making. Usually you will have made handle loops (see page 102) with rings attached so you can clip the piped handles onto the rings. Finish making up your bag and clip the hooks onto the rings of the handle loop.

1 **Fold and stitch the piped handle** – fold and pin the closed-end strap in half along its length to form a fabric tube. Measure and mark 5cm (2in) in from both short edges. Stitch the strap along the open edge with a 3mm (⅛in) seam allowance, starting and stopping your stitches at the 5cm (2in) markings. See **Fig a**.

Fig a *Stitch a fabric tube for the tubing. Stop and start stitching at the 5cm (2in) markings.*

a

2 **Stuff the handle** – insert one end of the flexi-tubing into the fabric tube. Stuff the tubing into the fabric tube until you reach the 5cm (2in) marking at the other end. Stitch a line of stitches perpendicular to the 5cm (2in) marking. See **Fig b**. Sew one line of stitches and stitch back over the line in reverse for extra strength. This will trap the tubing inside the handle. Repeat with the other 5cm (2in) marking.

3 **Attach the trigger hooks** – thread the ring of one of the trigger hooks onto one of the handle ends. Fold the fabric handle end over the ring by 2cm (¾in) so that the WS are touching and stitch the end down. Sew one line of stitches and stitch back over the line in reverse for extra strength. Repeat with the other hook and handle end. The handle is now ready to use.

b

Fig b *Stitch a line of stitches at 90 degrees to the 5cm (2in) markings.*

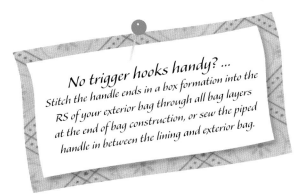

No trigger hooks handy? ...
Stitch the handle ends in a box formation into the RS of your exterior bag through all bag layers at the end of bag construction, or sew the piped handle in between the lining and exterior bag.

SIX IDEAS FOR 'UPCYCLING' ITEMS TO MAKE BAG HANDLES

⊛ Try plaiting three vintage scarves and tying metal rings on either end for a handle that will bring big impact to a plain bag.

⊛ Try weaving a vibrant chiffon scarf through a length of large-link chain for an instantly glam purse chain handle.

⊛ Try felting 100 per cent wool items (such as jumpers and scarves etc.). Simply wash the wool item in your washing machine at 60 degrees (or above) on a cottons cycle. You should be left with a dense felt-like fabric that has a lovely fuzzy texture and does not fray when cut. You may need to wash the item more than once to achieve the desired texture.

⊛ Try using chunky bangles for quick and eye-catching wristlet handles.

⊛ Try hunting around in charity shops or thrift shops for pre-owned bags and purses and take them apart for spares. If you're patient you can sometimes salvage some nice vintage bag hardware such as rings, purse locks, chain and, of course, bag handles.

⊛ Try snipping off fabric straps from old bags and then embellishing them with pretty vintage brooches for a 'shabby chic' mix-and-match look.

Ready-Made Handles

The range of ready-made bag handles has grown vastly. I remember the days when it was all just bamboo and plastic. Today, handbag handles are available in a wide choice of materials such as real and faux leather, metal chain, wood, acrylic and Lucite in all of the colours of the rainbow. Some even come with fancy metalware already attached. Bag makers are spoilt for choice!

WHY USE READY-MADE HANDLES?

◉ **Because they look great** – there are times when you want to make a bag that looks less homemade, and more 'handmade' (or maybe even shop-bought). Adding a smart-looking ready-made bag handle to your creation is an easy way to add a more polished and professional look to your bag. Even the most basic tote bag can be 'lifted' out of the ordinary by popping on a pair of ready-made handles (see page 25).

◉ **Because they are made for their purpose** – fabric straps have their limitations. Fabric straps may not always look right/perfect on your bag. Depending on the type of bag you are making you may need a handle that is longer, stronger, waterproof, or has fancy metal clips, rings or catches attached. There are even times when your bag fabric, when folded to make straps, is simply too thick for your sewing machine. At times like these ready-made handles are smart and stress-free alternatives to making your own handles.

◉ **Because you want to finish your bag** – if time is running out and you have a loved one waiting on their bag present, ready-made bag handles are extremely convenient!

Left Ready-made handles come in an amazing choice of colours, so there's bound to be one to match your fabric.

Types of ready-made handles

Handles can be categorized by their methods of application to your bags. Some ready-made handles require hand stitching onto your bag, while other handles can simply clipped on, and yet others require the use of fabric handle loops for example.

Sew-on handles These handles usually have pre-punched tab ends. Hand-sew these handles to the front of your bag (through all layers for extra strength) using backstitch and tapestry thread. You can also use doubled-over quality sewing thread, but it's not quite as strong or as attractive as tapestry thread.

Clip-on handles These handles or straps have strong metal clip ends. Ensure that you select handles with good quality clips, for obvious reasons. Good quality clip-on handles have metal clips that are almost too hard to squeeze together by hand and the clips should be set with metal teeth to grip the fabric. To apply these handles, place the clips over the top edge of your completed bag, cover the tips of a pair household pliers with a scrap of fabric (to protect the handles from scratches), and use the pliers to clamp the clips of the handles firmly shut over the bag fabric.

Trigger hook end handles These handles have trigger hooks attached to the ends. These types of handles are attached to your bag via fabric handle loops with D-rings (see page 102). Thread the D-rings onto the handle loops and stitch the handle loops (with D-rings attached) to the RS of the bag exterior before you sew the lining and the exterior together (see page 105).

Chain handles These handles are great for making your bags look expensive and they are perfect for adding instant flash and sparkle to evening and special occasion bags. To attach chain handles you need metal rings (attached to handle loops, see page 102) on your bag. To thread the end links of the chain to the handle loop rings you can either use pliers to prize the end links open, or you can add trigger hooks to the ends or the chain so the chain can be clipped on and off (see page 60).

Make it...
The Great Getaway Bag

This is one travel bag that is sure to get admiring glances at the train station, airport or hotel. Very roomy, practical, and totally pretty, this bag will haul your holiday gear in style, and it fits into the overhead locker on the plane too. A nice wide flat base makes the bag easy to see into and to pack, and lots of pockets help keep your luggage organized. This bag is an investment make – use your favourite brightest fabrics and set aside some evenings to make a professional-looking bag that you'll love to use again and again.

Front view *Perfect for those who can't travel light, this bag will carry loads. But thanks to its soft structure you can take it on the plane with you.*

Side view *The roomy front pocket is perfect for your travel essentials such as passport, book and MP3 player.*

Interior *Inside, the bag is nice and wide and the pockets help you to keep things under control.*

NEED TO KNOW

⊛ In this bag, the woven fusible interfacing is applied to the exterior fabric. The fusible fleece is applied to the lining fabric.

⊛ If you are making an oilcloth version of this bag, only pin in the seam allowances, use a non-stick sewing foot, and only iron the fabric with a pressing cloth using a gentle heat. Also, you won't need fusible interfacing for the oilcloth.

⊛ This bag makes uses a box top zip, so called because it gives you a nice and wide top and side edge which is perfect for larger and boxier bags (see page 90).

⊛ All seam allowances are 1cm (3/8in) unless stated.

⊛ Pattern pieces are given in the pull-out section and include the 1cm (3/8in) seam allowance.

You will need

- 1 piece of home dec fabric for exterior, 1m (1yd) x 137cm (54in)
- 1 piece of home dec fabric for lining, 1.25m (1¼yd) x 137cm (54in)
- 1 piece of home dec fabric for trim, strap and pocket tab, 50cm (½yd) x 137cm (54in)
- Sewing threads to match the fabrics
- Single-sided fusible fleece, 1.5m (1½yd)
- Woven fusible interfacing, 1.5m (1½yd)
- Magnetic snap closure, 18mm (¾in)
- Chunky nylon zip (for the box top zip), 80cm (31½in)
- Nylon zip (for the flush zip pocket), 18cm (7in)
- Flexi-tube for making piped handles, 76cm (30in), OR a pair of ready-made piped handles, 45cm (17¾in)
- Strap slider, 4cm (1½in)
- 3 rectangular rings, 4cm (1½in) wide
- Large size grid bag bottom
- 6 bag feet (optional)
- Hand-sewing needle
- Disappearing marker
- Seam ripper
- Cotton or linen pressing cloth

Preparation

Cut the fabric and interfacing pieces as follows:

From The Great Getaway Bag (main body) pattern piece (see pull-out section)

- 2 x exterior fabric
- 2 x fusible interfacing
- 2 x lining fabric
- 2 x fusible fleece

From The Great Getaway Bag (front and lining pocket) pattern piece (see pull-out section)

- 1 x exterior fabric
- 1 x fusible interfacing
- 2 x lining fabric
- 1 x fusible fleece

From The Great Getaway Bag (front pocket flap) pattern piece (see pull-out section)

- 1 x exterior fabric
- 1 x fusible interfacing
- 1 x lining fabric
- 1 x fusible fleece

From The Great Getaway Bag (corner trim) pattern piece (see pull-out section)

- 2 x exterior trim fabric

Then turn the pattern over to cut:

- 2 x exterior fabric (in mirror image)

From The Great Getaway Bag (zip top panels for the box top zip) pattern piece (see pull-out section)

- 1 x exterior fabric
- 1 x fusible interfacing
- 1 x lining fabric
- 1 x fusible fleece

Then turn the pattern over to cut:

- 1 x exterior fabric (in mirror image)
- 1 x fusible interfacing (in mirror image)
- 1 x lining fabric (in mirror image)
- 1 x fusible fleece (in mirror image)

From The Great Getaway Bag (zip bottom panels for the box top zip) pattern piece (see pull-out section)

- 2 x exterior fabric
- 2 x fusible interfacing
- 2 x lining fabric
- 2 x fusible fleece

Transfer all pattern notches and markings to the fabric with a disappearing marker

Also cut:

- 1 piece of exterior fabric, 2 pieces of lining fabric, and 1 piece each of fusible interfacing and fusible fleece, 51 x 27cm (20 x 10⅝in), for the bag base
- 2 pieces of lining fabric, 26 x 20cm (10¼ x 8in), for the flush zip pocket
- 2 pieces of exterior trim fabric, 75 x 14cm (29½ x 5½in), for the adjustable strap
- 1 piece of exterior trim fabric, 36 x 14cm (14⅛ x 5½in), for the handle loops, pocket tab and pocket tab loop
- 2 pieces of fusible interfacing, 5cm (2in) square, for the handle loop reinforcement
- 2 pieces of fusible interfacing, 2.5cm (1in) square, for the magnetic snap reinforcement
- 2 pieces of fusible interfacing, 23 x 5cm (9 x 2in), for the handle reinforcement
- 2 pieces of exterior trim fabric, 50 x 6cm (19½ x 2⅜in) to make piped handles (if using)
- 2 pieces of exterior trim fabric, 9 x 5cm (3½ x 2in) for the zip ends for the box top zip
- 2 pieces of exterior trim fabric, 6 x 4cm (2⅜ x 1½in) for the zip pulls for the box top zip

Stay organized ...
There are quite a few pieces to this bag. To prevent confusion it's worth labelling each piece as you cut it and ironing the interfacing pieces to their appropriate fabric pieces as soon as they are cut.

Interfacing, strap and handles and zip preparation

1 **Interface the exterior and lining fabric pieces** – match the fusible interfacing pattern pieces to their partner exterior fabric pieces and iron them to the WS of the exterior fabric pieces. Then match the fusible fleece pattern pieces to their partner lining fabric pieces and iron them to the WS of the lining fabric pieces.

2 **Make the handle loops** – take the handle loop/pocket tab fabric and cut off a 20cm (8in) piece. Divide that piece into two equal lengths and follow the steps on page 103 to make two closed-end straps. Thread a rectangular ring onto each of the handle loops.

Below *The long, adjustable strap will make this bag a breeze to carry on your travels, either on your shoulder or cross-body for a truly hands-free experience.*

Fig a Stitch the handle loop in a box formation, you can also stitch an 'X' in the box if desired.

3 **Stitch the handle loops to the exterior zip top panels** – take one of the zip top panel pieces RSU (with the straight long edge on the left) and make a mark in the centre of the panel 18cm (7in), up from the short bottom edge. Take one of the handle loop interfacing pieces RSU and iron it to the WS of the zip top panel piece behind the mark you have just made. Turn the zip top panel piece RSU and take one of the handle loops (folded in half with rectangular ring attached and pointing upwards) and place it onto one of the handle loop pattern markings on the RS exterior zip top panel piece. Pin in place and stitch to the panel in a box formation for strength. See **Fig a**. Repeat with the other handle loop and zip top panel piece.

4 **Make the adjustable strap** – bring the two pieces of strap fabric RST, pin and stitch along one of the short edges to make one long strap. Iron the seam open and follow the steps on page 103 to make one closed-end strap (which forms the basis of an adjustable strap).

5 **Make the piped bag handles** – (if using), take the flexi-tube and divide it into two equal lengths. Take the piped handle fabric pieces and follow the steps on page 109 to make two piped handles (but do not add trigger hooks to the handles).

6 **Make the zip pulls** – fold one of the zip pull fabric pieces in half by bringing the short edges RST, stitch along both side edges and clip the corners. Turn RSO and iron. Repeat with the other zip pull fabric piece.

7 **Stitch the zip ends to the zip** – take one of the zip end fabric pieces RSU, fold under one of the short edges 1cm (⅜in) and iron the fold. Place the zip end RSU onto one of the centre RS short edges of the zip. Match up the raw edges of the zip end with the short edge of the zip. Topstitch the zip end to the zip along the folded edge 3mm (⅛in) from the edge (see step 1 on page 86). Repeat with the other zip end.

The bag exterior

8 Stitch the corner trims to bottom of the bag – take one the corner trim pieces WSU and fold the curved edge in 1cm (⅜in) to the WS and iron the fold. Clip the curve, turn the trim RSU and match the raw edges on the bottom and side edges of the trim to a RS bottom corner of one the exterior main body pieces. Pin and topstitch the trim to the exterior all around the trim with a 3mm (⅛in) seam allowance. Repeat with the other three corner trim pieces, but ensure you place two of the corner trims onto the RS of the exterior pocket piece. See **Fig b**.

9 Make the exterior pocket tab – take the handle loop/ pocket tab fabric, cut off a 10cm (4in) piece and follow step 2 of closed-end straps on page 103. Completely open out the tab and mark an 'X' for the magnetic snap 2cm (¾in) up from the bottom edge fold. See **Fig c**. Iron one of the magnetic snap fusible reinforcement pieces onto the WS of the tab over the 'X' mark and apply the non-magnetic part of the snap by following step 2 of magnetic snap on page 91. Fold up the tab and topstitch all around 3mm (⅛in) from the edge.

10 Make the pocket tab loop – take the remainder of the handle loop/pocket tab fabric and follow the steps on page 102 to make one open-end strap. Thread on the last rectangular ring, fold the strap in half and stitch on the strap close to the rectangular ring to trap it in the centre of the loop. Take the pocket tab WSU (with magnetic snap inserted) and fold the free edge 2cm (¾in) over the ring of the tab loop. Topstitch the end down 3mm (⅛in) from the edge.

b

Fig b *Pin and stitch two corner trims to one bag exterior piece and stitch the other two corner trims to the exterior pocket piece.*

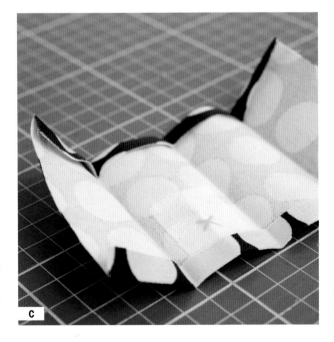

c

Pipe dreams ...
If you are a more experienced sewist (and your sewing machine can handle the extra layers), you can insert some attractive piping in the top and side seams of this bag (see pages 144–145). The result would look fab!

Fig c *Unfold the closed-end strap fabric and mark an 'X' for the magnetic snap half as shown.*

11 **Make the exterior pocket flap** – take the pocket tab loop WSU (folded in half with pocket tab attached) and place it onto the pocket tab loop pattern marking on the RS pocket flap exterior fabric piece. See **Fig d**. Match up the raw edges of the pocket tab loop and the pocket flap fabric. Hold the pocket tab loop in place with your fingers and stitch with a 5mm (³⁄₁₆in) seam allowance. Bring the exterior and lining pocket fabric flap pieces RST, pin and stitch all around the flap leaving a gap of 15cm (6in) in the top edge for turning out. Clip the corners, iron the seams open and turn RSO. Push the seams of the gap into the hole and iron the folds to get a straight edge along the top of the flap.

12 **Make the exterior pocket** – take the exterior pocket piece RSU and follow the step 2 on page 91 to insert the magnetic part of the snap into the snap pattern marking. Bring the exterior and lining pocket pieces RST. Match the raw top edges, pin and stitch along the top edge only. Iron the seam open, flip the exterior layer over to the RS, iron and topstitch along the top edge 3mm (⅛in) from the edge.

13 **Stitch the exterior pocket and flap to the bag** – take the exterior pocket and place it RSU onto the RS exterior main body fabric piece (which has no corner trims). Match up the raw bottom and side edges of the pocket and the main body piece, pin and stitch along the sides and bottom with a 5mm (³⁄₁₆in) seam allowance. Place the top edge of the pocket flap RSU onto the RS exterior, 2cm (¾in) up from the top edge of the pocket. Ensure the flap is straight and central (and the pocket tab clicks into place onto the magnetic snap). Pin and topstitch the pocket flap in place along the top edge 3mm (⅛in) from the edge – stitching the gap in the flap shut as you sew.

14 **Stitch the bag handles to the exterior** – take the handle interfacing pieces and iron them to the WS of the exterior main body fabric pieces behind the pattern markings for the handles. If using your handmade piped handles, take the handle RSU and stitch the handle tabs to the RS exterior in a box formation for strength. Repeat with the other handle. If using ready-made handles stitch the tabs to the exterior fabric through the pre-punched holes.

Right *An exterior pocket on travel bags is so handy for keeping those bits and pieces you need to access quickly on your journey!*

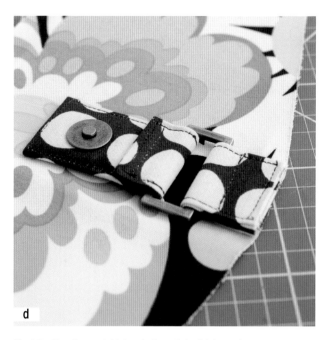

d

Fig d *Position the pocket tab onto the exterior fabric as shown.*

The box top zip (exterior)

15 **Stitch the zip top panels to the zip** – bring one of the zip top panel fabric pieces and the zip RST. Match up the long edge of the zip – you'll see that the zip is longer than the zip top panels (and that is fine), match up the centre long edge of the zip and the centre long edge of the zip top panel before pinning both together. Stitch the panel to the zip with a 5mm (³⁄₁₆in) seam allowance. Repeat with the other zip top panel piece and other zip side.

16 **Stitch the zip pulls to the zip bottom panels** – fold the zip bottom panels in half WST widthways and iron the fold. Take one of the zip pulls (with raw edge facing up) and place it in the centre folded top edge of the bottom panel. Match the edges, pin and stitch in place with a 5mm (³⁄₁₆in) seam allowance. See **Fig e**. Repeat with the other zip pull.

17 **Stitch the zip bottom panels to the zip top panel** – take a zip bottom panel WSU and place the folded edge onto the RS short edge of the zip top panel (with zip inserted). Match the edges, pin and stitch the bottom panel to the zip with a 1cm (³⁄₈in) seam allowance. Turn RSU, fold the bottom panel down to the RS and iron the fold. If the fabric thickness allows, topstitch along the fold on the bottom panel 3mm (⅛in) from the edge. See **Fig f**. Repeat with the other bottom panel.

e

Fig e This clever zip pull will give you something to grab while opening and closing the bag, thus making the zip easier to use.

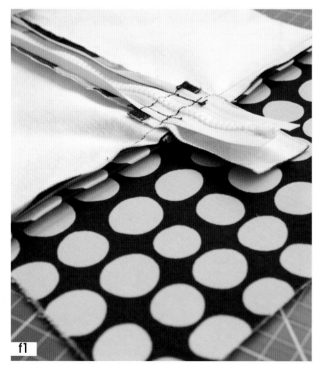

f1

f2

Fig f1–f2 View from the WS: stitch the zip bottom panel and the zip top panel RST. View from the RS: fold the zip bottom panel down.

Assembling the bag exterior

18 Stitch the exterior zip top panel and main body pieces together – bring the zip top panel (with zip and zip bottom panels inserted) and the main body pieces RST. Take care to match the top edges of the corner trim and the zip bottom panel – both should form a smooth line that appears to run from the bag side to the bag front/back bottom corner. See **Fig g**. Pin and stitch together along the top and side edges stopping 1cm (⅜in) up from the bottom edge – sew several securing stitches at both ends. Repeat with the other exterior main body piece.

19 Stitch the exterior bag base to the exterior bag – bring the short edges of the exterior bag and the exterior base RST, pin and stitch – stopping and starting 1cm from the edge (sewing securing stitches at both ends as in step 18). Repeat for the long edges of the base and bag. Clip off the corners.

20 Insert the bag feet into the base – (if using) if not using bag feet proceed to step 21. Mark the position of the bag feet on the RS of the bag base 1.5cm (½in) in from the edge. Use a seam ripper to make tiny incisions for each prong in the markings. Take one of the bag feet and push the prongs through a bag foot marking through RS of the bag base and press the prongs down to secure. Repeat for the other bag feet.

The bag lining

21 Insert the flush zip pocket into the lining – take the smaller zip and the two flush zip pocket fabric pieces and follow steps 2–8 on pages 67–69 to insert a flush zip pocket into the centre of the one of the lining main body pieces 7cm (2¾in) down from the top edge.

22 Measure and mark the lining pocket divider lines – take the large lining pocket piece RSU and fold the top edge of the pocket down 1cm (⅜in) to the WS, iron and repeat. Stitch the fold down 5mm (³⁄₁₆in) from the top edge. Mark one or more pocket divider lines where desired onto the pocket fabric. See step 11, page 80.

23 Stitch the lining pocket to the main body lining pieces – place the pocket RSU onto the RS of the other lining main body piece (which has no pocket). Match up the bottom and side edges of the pocket and the main body piece and pin. Stitch the pocket to the main body piece along the divider line(s) and then stitch along the bottom and side edges of the pocket with a 5mm (³⁄₁₆in) seam allowance.

g

Fig g *Take care to match the top zip bottom panel with the top of the bottom corner so it will look as if one is flowing into the other.*

The box top zip (lining)

24 Assemble the bag lining (top, body and sides) – take one of the lining zip top panels RSU and fold the long straight edge down 1cm (⅜in) to the WS and iron the fold. Repeat with the other lining zip top panel. Assemble the lining in the same way as the bag exterior (steps 17–18) except there is no zip to insert. See **Fig h**.

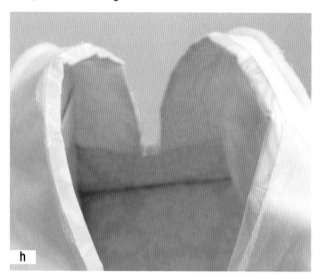

Fig h *Make up the bag lining in the same way as for the bag exterior except there is no zip or zip parts to insert. You should be left with a lining bag that has a long thin rectangular hole along the top.*

25 Stitch the lining base to the lining bag – the lining base is made of two layers, which will form a pocket into which the bag bottom is inserted. Bring the two lining base fabric pieces WS together, match up all edges and treat as one layer. With the interfaced lining base piece uppermost, stitch the lining base to the lining bag in the same way as for the exterior bag in step 19, except you need to leave one of the short edges of the base open.

26 Insert the bag bottom into the lining – measure the width and the length of the lining (seam to seam). Subtract 5mm (³⁄₁₆in) from both measurements – this will be the measurement of the grid bag bottom. Cut the grid bag bottom to size and trim off the corner tips. Slide the bag bottom into the lining through the opening and stitch the gap shut. See **Fig i**.

Assembling the bag

27 Stitch the lining base to the exterior base – open the zip on the exterior bag. Choose which side (front or back) you prefer to have the flush zip pocket in the bag lining and then bring together the lining base and the exterior base WST. Match all edges, pin and stitch all around with a 5mm (³⁄₁₆in) seam allowance. Turn the bag RSO by reaching into the zip hole of the exterior bag and peeling the exterior bag back over the lining bag. See **Fig j**.

Fig j1–j2 *Place the lining bag base WS onto the exterior base WS, match all edges and stitch together in the seam allowance approx 5mm (³⁄₁₆in) from the edge; turn the exterior bag RSO over the lining bag by peeling it back like a banana skin.*

Fig i *Slide the grid bag bottom into the lining base and stitch the hole shut. For best results ensure that it is a snug fit.*

Box top zip – final assembly

28 Stitch the lining and exterior side top and side seams together – bring together the side and top edge seams of the lining and exterior bags and hand stitch them together in the seam allowance. See **Fig k**. Start and stop sewing 15cm (6in) up from the bottom edge. Repeat on the other side.

Fig k *Hand stitch the top and side seams of the lining and the exterior bag together. Don't worry too much about making the stitches neat, as they won't be on show.*

29 Stitch the lining zip opening to the zip – match the folded edge of the lining zip opening to the fabric of the zip. Hand stitch together with small and neat stitches. See **Fig l**.

30 Finishing touches – attach the adjustable strap to the bag following steps 2–3 on pages 106–107 and go and pack your bags!

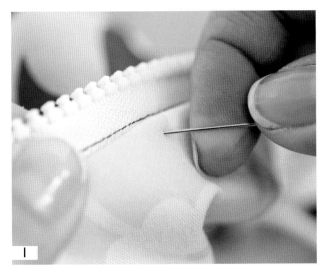

Fig l *Hand sew the folded edge of the lining to the fabric of the zip. To make life easier, lift the fabric of the zip away from the exterior seam so you only have one layer to sew through.*

Above *The spotty version is made from fantastic wipe-clean oilcloth, great for whisking away the marks and bumps your luggage tends to pick up on your travels. It also makes a great water resistant holdall for sporting activities.*

7: POCKETS

Well-placed and plentiful pockets in your bags help keep you calm and collected when you're in a hurry or when your arms are full. The last thing you need at a busy checkout is to have to send a search party into your bag for your money. Pockets can look as fun or pretty as they are functional. This chapter looks at various types of pockets and their methods of construction and lining. It also explains how you can combine fastenings with your pockets in order to make them extra secure. Zip pockets are covered in the Linings chapter starting on page 64 (and turn to page 83 for advice on adding zips in general). The table below reveals some of the more commonly used pockets, their benefits and uses.

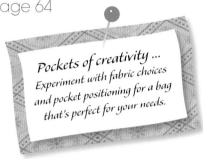

Pockets of creativity ...
Experiment with fabric choices and pocket positioning for a bag that's perfect for your needs.

POCKET TYPE	BENEFITS	SUGGESTED USES
Slip Pocket: page 124	Flat profile, therefore suitable for all bags, fast to make and utilizes a minimal amount of fabric.	Great for linings of slimline evening purses/clutches or place on the exterior for fast access to non-precious items.
Lined Slip Pocket: page 125	As above plus metal closures can be applied to this pocket type. Two different fabrics provide an excuse to inject more colour.	As above.
Bellows Pocket: page 126	Clever because they lie flat when empty, but expand outwards to accommodate your gear. Metal closures can be added for extra security. Best for bulky items.	Great for the exterior of larger casual bags or structured satchels. Also good for the lining of organizer-style bags, totes or picnic bags.
Elasticized-Top Pocket: page 128	An easy access pocket with the added control and security of a cinched-in top edge. Best for bulky items.	Great on the exterior of larger bags (such as travel bags or hold-alls) for storing taller items. Also good for the lining of organizer-style bags, nappy or messenger bags.
Darted-Corner Pocket: page 130	A box-shaped pocket that looks very professional. Provides quick and easy access. Can have a flap and metal closures can be added if desired. Best for bulky items.	Attractive enough for the exterior of smarter daytime bags (such as work/ city day-tripper bags) but equally great on larger casual bags (such as weekender or gym bags).

Slip Pocket A basic pocket and one of the easiest types to make. As this pocket is flat in profile you can put it into the daintiest of purses without adding any bulk to the purse. See page 124.

Lined Slip Pocket Another flat profile pocket that is very simple to make. These pockets look more attractive than slip pockets because the two pocket fabrics can echo the bag exterior fabric and the lining fabric. See page 125.

Bellows Pocket These pockets have in-built capacity at the sides so you can stuff more things into the pocket without cluttering up the overall look of your bag. See pages 126–127.

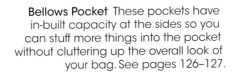

Elasticized-Top Pocket This voluminous pocket is very handy when you want easy access to your gear. The elastic top grips taller items such as bottles or umbrellas, keeping them flush against your bag. See pages 128–129.

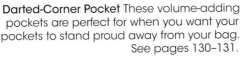

Darted-Corner Pocket These volume-adding pockets are perfect for when you want your pockets to stand proud away from your bag. See pages 130–131.

Slip Pocket

This is the most basic of pockets to make. It has a completely flat profile making it very suitable for small evening bags, for example. As these pockets are unlined they are best suited to fabrics that are the same colour on both sides (self-coloured).

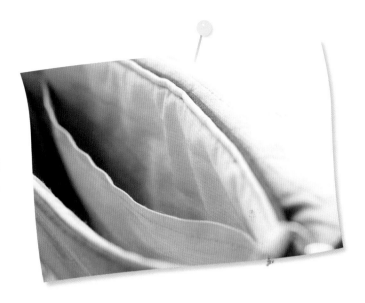

You will need

- 1 piece of self-coloured fabric. To gauge the width and height of your pocket fabric piece see Need To Know

Metal-free zone ...

Because this pocket is unlined it is not suitable for the addition of metal fastenings, though there's nothing stopping you from adding a loop and button fastening (see page 42).

NEED TO KNOW

⊕ To gauge the width of your pocket fabric decide how wide you want your finished pocket and add 2cm (¾in). If you want your finished pocket to be 18cm (7in) wide, your pocket fabric needs to be 22cm (8⅝in) wide.

⊕ To gauge the height of your pocket decide on the height of your finished pocket and add 2cm (¾in). If you want your finished pocket to be 15cm (6in) high, your pocket fabric needs to be 19cm (7½in) high.

⊕ All seam allowances are 1cm (⅜in) unless stated otherwise.

⊕ Make up pockets and stitch them to your bag fabric BEFORE constructing your bags.

1 **Prepare and fold your pocket fabric** – fold both the side edges in 1cm (⅜in) and iron the folds. Fold the side edges in 1cm (⅜in) again and iron the folds. Repeat the process in the same way with the top and bottom edges. See **Fig a**. Topstitch along the top edge of the pocket 5mm (³⁄₁₆in) away from the edge.

2 **Pin and stitch the pocket to your bag** – choose the position of your pocket on your bag lining/exterior. With the pocket folds facing down, pin into position nice and straight. Stitch the pocket in place along the bottom and side edges with a 3mm (⅛in) seam allowance. See **Fig b**. If your pocket is wide enough you can run a line of stitches into your pocket to make a central divider if desired.

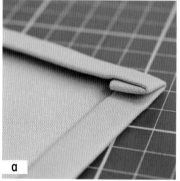

Fig a *Fold in the top and bottom edges 1cm (⅜in) and press. Repeat the process.*

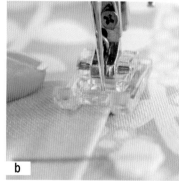

Fig b *Stitch the pocket in place with a 3mm (⅛in) seam allowance.*

Lined Slip Pocket

This is the second most basic of pockets to make. It has a completely flat profile making it very suitable for small evening bags, for example. As these pockets are lined you can add a magnetic snap closure if desired (see page 91).

You will need

- 1 piece of lining fabric
- 1 piece of exterior fabric. To gauge the width and height of both your fabric pieces see Need To Know
- Set of magnetic snaps (optional – see tip)

NEED TO KNOW

- To gauge the width of your pocket fabric decide how wide you want your finished pocket and add 4cm (1½in). If you want your finished pocket to be 18cm (7in) wide, your pocket fabric needs to be 22cm (8⅝in) wide.
- To gauge the height of your pocket decide on the height of your finished pocket and add 4cm (1½in). If you want your finished pocket to be 15cm (6in) high, your pocket fabric needs to be 19cm (7½in) high.
- All seam allowances are 1cm (⅜in) unless stated otherwise.
- Make up pockets and stitch them to your bag fabric BEFORE constructing your bags.

1 Prepare the pocket for the magnetic snap – if you are not using a magnetic snap proceed to step 2. Take one of the pocket fabric pieces and mark the magnetic snap position – I prefer mine to be at least 3cm (1⅛in) down from the raw top edge. Then insert the non-magnetic half of the snap into the pocket RS lining by following the steps on page 91. Insert the magnetic half of the snap into the pocket position on the bag lining/exterior fabric piece.

2 Assemble the pocket – bring the two pocket fabric pieces RST, pin and stitch all around the bottom and side edges, but leave a gap in the bottom edge of at least 9cm (3½in) for turning out. Clip off the corners of the pocket. Iron the seams open and turn the pocket RSO through the gap. Push the raw edges of the gap into the hole and iron the pocket. See **Fig a**.

3 Pin and stitch the pocket to your bag – choose the position of the pocket on your bag lining/exterior. If you are using a magnetic snap click the snap halves on the pocket and the bag fabric piece together. Pin the pocket into position nice and straight. Stitch the pocket in place along the bottom and side edges of the pocket, stitching the gap shut as you sew. See **Fig b**.

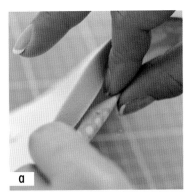

a

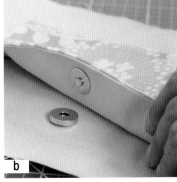

b

Fig a *After you have turned your pocket RSO, push the raw edges of the gap into the hole so that the edges are aligned. Iron the pocket.*

Fig b *And there you have it – one neat lined slip pocket. This one even has a handy magnetic snap closure.*

Pocket protection ...
If adding a magnetic snap to the pocket lining it is a good idea to interface/ interline your pocket fabric to protect it from repeated pulling (see page 91).

Bellows Pocket

This pocket has the benefit of added volume so you can store more in the pocket without disturbing the profile of the bag. As these pockets are lined you can add a magnetic snap closure if desired.

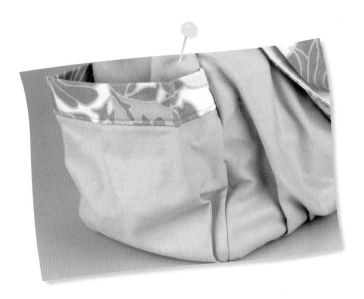

You will need

- 1 piece of lining fabric
- 1 piece of exterior fabric. To gauge the width and height of both your fabric pieces see Need To Know
- Set of magnetic snaps (optional – see tip on page 125)
- Ruler
- Disappearing marker

NEED TO KNOW

- To gauge the width of your fabric decide how wide you want the front panel of your bellows pocket to be, and then decide how wide you'd like the sides of the pocket to be, finally add on two lots of seam allowance. If your seam allowance is 1cm (⅜in) and you want a bellows pocket that is 10cm (4in) wide and 4cm (1½in) deep, the calculation is:

  1 x 10cm (4in) + 2 x 4cm (1½in) + 2 x 1cm (⅜in) = total bellows pocket fabric width of 20cm (8in).

- To gauge the height of your pocket decide on the height of your finished pocket and add on two lots of seam allowance. If you want your finished pocket to be 15cm (6in) high, your pocket fabric needs to be 17cm (6⅝in) high.

- All seam allowances are 1cm (⅜in) unless stated otherwise.

- Make up pockets and stitch them to your bag fabric BEFORE constructing your bags.

Pocket placement ...
You can stitch this pocket as high up on your bag as desired, or you may prefer the pocket to sit right at the bottom of your bag – the choice is yours.

1 **Fold and concertina pleat the pocket sides** – follow steps 1 and 2 of lined slip pockets on page 125. With the pocket RSU, measure and mark the fold lines for the bellows and then fold under the side edges at the fold marks. Returning to the example in the Need To Know box: in the top and bottom centre edge of the pocket make two marks 10cm (4in) apart. Then fold under both side edges at the marks and iron the folds to form the pocket side panels. After the side panels have been formed, fold the side panels in half (concertina style) to form the bellows. Finally, topstitch a third of the way down along the front side edge folds to ensure the bellows folds remain crisp and sharp on the pocket. See **Fig a**.

Pockets too thick? ...
If you want to make unlined bellows pockets (because you are working with thick fabric) take one pocket fabric piece and follow step 1 on page 124 before returning here to step 1 to measure and mark the fold lines.

a1

a2

a3

Fig a1–a3 *Fold under the side edges to form the side panels for the pocket, then fold the side panels in half like a concertina pleat and finally topstitch a third of the pocket height down from the pocket side top edges.*

2 **Pin and stitch the pocket to your bag (up from the bottom of the bag)** – choose the position of your pocket on your bag lining/exterior. If you are using a magnetic snap, then click the snap halves on the pocket and your bag fabric piece together. Pin the pocket into position, nice and straight. As you pin ensure the side pleats also run straight and even all the way down. Stitch the pocket in place along the bottom and side edges stitching the bottom gap shut as you sew. See **Fig b**.

3 **Alternatively, pin and stitch the pocket to your bag (to the bag bottom)** – follow step 2 but stitch the pocket in place along the side edges of the pocket only. The bottom edge of the pocket will be sewn into the bottom seam of the bag at a later stage when you construct the bag.

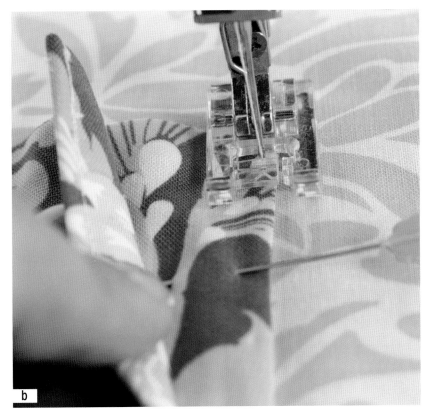

b

Fig b *As you stitch the side edges of the pocket, ensure you keep the side pleats out of the way.*

Elasticized-Top Pocket

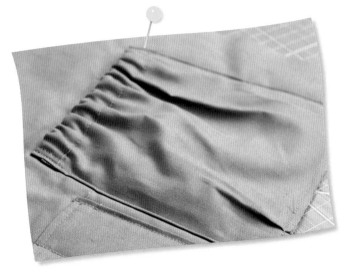

This pocket has the benefit of a narrower elasticized top edge so the pocket contents stay put when you're running for the bus. It is also great for keeping the contents under control – perfect for storing baby bottles, for example.

You will need

- 1 piece of lining fabric
- 1 piece of exterior fabric. To gauge the width and height of both your fabric pieces see Need To Know
- 1 piece of elastic as wide as the width of your pocket fabric
- Safety pin or bodkin
- Ruler
- Disappearing marker

NEED TO KNOW

- To gauge the width of your pocket fabric decide how wide you want your pocket to be when fully extended then add 2cm (¾in). If you want your finished pocket to be 15cm (6in) wide (fully extended), your pocket fabric needs to be 17cm (6⅝in) wide.
- To gauge the height of your pocket decide on the height of your finished pocket and add 4cm (1½in). If you want your finished pocket to be 15cm (6in) high, your pocket fabric needs to be 19cm (7½in) high.
- All seam allowances are 1cm (⅜in) unless stated otherwise.
- Make up pockets and stitch them to your bag fabric BEFORE constructing your bags.

1 **Create a channel for the elastic** – bring the two pocket fabric pieces RST, pin and stitch along the top edge. Iron the seams open and flip one of the fabric pieces over so that the RS of the pocket is facing out. Stitch a single line of stitches close to the top edge to form a channel tall enough to accommodate the elastic (see tip). See **Fig a**.

Channel tunnel ...
The height of the elastic channel needs to be 1cm (⅜in) taller than the height of your elastic.

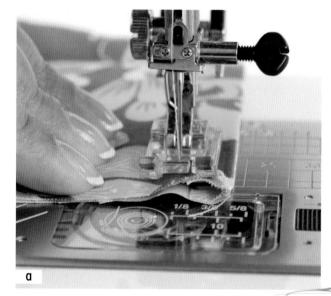

a

Fig a *Stitch a line of stitches along the top of the pocket to create a channel that is tall enough for your elastic.*

Fig b *Pull on the elastic and gather the pocket fabric. Test the pocket to get the desired stretchiness and trim off the excess elastic when satisfied.*

2 **Insert the elastic** – measure and mark 2.5cm (1in) in from both the channel sides. Attach the safety pin/bodkin to one of the elastic ends and use it to thread the elastic through the channel. Pull the elastic out at the other end of the channel and remove the safety pin/bodkin. Feeling through the fabric with your fingers, pull the elastic back into the channel until the end almost reaches the 2.5cm (1in) channel mark. Stitch across the elastic (through both pocket fabric layers) at the 2.5cm (1in) channel mark to secure the elastic end in place.

3 **Gather your pocket fabric and cut the elastic to size** – take hold of the free end of the elastic and gather up the pocket fabric to your desired pocket width. Test the stretchiness of the elastic. See **Fig b**. The elastic should be tight enough to prevent your pocket from gaping open, but not so tight that the pocket will pull on the bag fabric. When you are happy with the elastic width, trim off the excess elastic and gently allow the elastic to slide back though the channel – almost up to the 2.5cm (1in) channel mark. Stitch the elastic end down as in step 2.

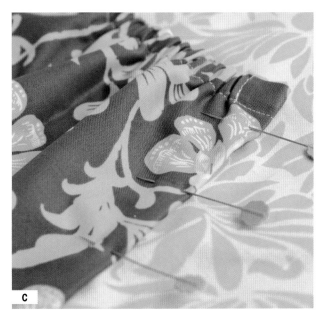

Fig c *The pocket is pinned into position on the bag fabric piece. Provided the pocket looks symmetrical on either side it's fine if the pocket sides lean inwards a little (due to the elasticized top).*

4 **Fold in the sides and stitch the pocket to your bag (up from the bottom of the bag)** – match the raw edges of the pocket, pin and stitch a zigzag stitch along the bottom and side edges to prevent fraying. Fold both side edges in 1cm (⅜in) and iron the folds. Repeat for the bottom edge. With the pocket folds facing down, pin the pocket into position, nice and straight. See **Fig c**. Stitch the pocket in place along the bottom and side edges.

5 **Alternatively, pin and stitch the pocket to your bag (to the bag bottom)** – fold in the side edges of the pocket as in step 4 and pin the pocket RSU to the bottom edge of your bag. Stitch the pocket in place along the pocket side edges only. The bottom edge of the pocket will be sewn into the bottom seam

Darted-Corner Pocket

This technique is perfect when you want a structural 3D pocket. The bottom corner darts add a boxy shape to the pocket so it stands proud away from your bag. You can make a flap for the pocket with any fastening. This style of pocket is usually placed up and away from the bottom of your bag. A square or rectangular shape works best.

You will need

- 1 piece of lining fabric for the pocket and flap (if making)
- 1 piece of exterior fabric for the pocket and flap (if making). To gauge the width and height of both pocket fabric pieces see Need To Know
- Ruler
- Disappearing marker
- Your choice of fastener (if making a flap)

NEED TO KNOW

- To gauge the width of your pocket fabric decide how wide you want the front panel of your pocket to be, and then decide how wide you'd like the sides of the pocket to be, finally add on two lots of seam allowance. If your seam allowance is 1cm (⅜in) and you want a darted pocket that is 10cm wide (4in) and 4cm (1½in) deep, the calculation is: 1 x 10cm (4in) + 2 x 4cm (1½in) + 2 x 1cm (⅜in) = total darted-corner pocket fabric width of 20cm (8in).

- To gauge the height of your pocket decide on the height of your finished pocket and add two lots of seam allowance. If you want your finished pocket to be 15cm (6in) high, your pocket fabric needs to be 17cm (6⅝in) high.

- To gauge the height of the pocket flap fabric decide on the height of your pocket flap and add 3cm (1⅛in). If you want your finished pocket flap to be 7cm (2¾in) high, your pocket flap fabric needs to be 10cm (4in) high.

- The width of your pocket flap (if making) should be the same as the pocket fabric width.

- Make up pockets and stitch them to your bag fabric BEFORE constructing your bags.

1 **Insert any fastenings** – if using, insert any fastenings to the RS of the exterior pocket fabric piece (see pages 91–93). I like to place my pocket fastenings at least 3cm (1⅛in) down from the raw top edge of the pocket fabric.

2 **Insert darts into the pocket** – follow steps 1–2 on pages 48–49 to insert darts into the bottom corners of the pocket exterior piece and the lining pieces. See **Fig a**.

Fig a *Insert darts into the bottom corner of both pocket fabric pieces.*

a

3 **Assemble the pocket** – bring your pocket lining/exterior pieces RST. Match up the bottom and side edges paying extra attention to the dart lines to ensure that they match. See **Fig b**. Pin and stitch all around the bottom and side edges, but leave a gap of at least 7cm (2¾in) in the bottom edge for turning out. Iron the seams flat and turn the pocket RSO through the gap in the pocket, push the raw edges of the gap into the hole and iron the entire pocket.

4 **Stitch the pocket to your bag** – place the pocket onto the bag fabric and mould and form the pocket so it sits like a 3D box shape. Ensure the pocket is sitting nice and straight and pin into position. Topstitch the pocket in place along the bottom and side edges, stitching the gap in the bottom edge shut as you sew. See **Fig c**.

5 **Make up the pocket flap** – if using, insert your chosen fastenings into the flap lining fabric (see pages 91–93). To test if the fastening position is suitable, place the flap lining fabric over your pocket. Bring the flap fabric pieces RST, pin and stitch all around, but leave a sufficient gap in the top edge for turning out. Clip any curves, iron the seams open, turn the flap RSO through the gap, and push the raw edges of the gap into the hole. Iron the flap and pin into position just above your pocket, at least 1cm (⅜in) above the top edge. Stitch the flap to your bag fabric along the flap top edge, stitching the gap shut as you sew. See **Fig d**.

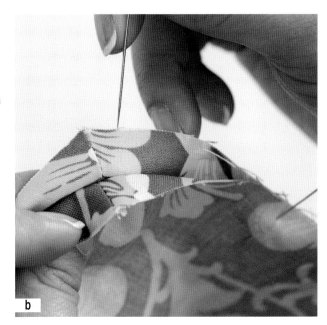

b

Fig b *The lining and exterior pieces are pinned together and the darts on both sides match.*

Fastening fun ...
If making a pocket flap, a fastening can be applied to the exterior pocket fabric piece. You could use a magnetic snap (see page 91), an invisible snap (see page 91) or a twist lock (see page 92).

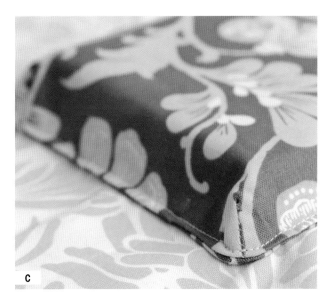

c

Fig c *The pocket stitched into position on the bag fabric. The pocket should resemble a box sitting on your bag fabric.*

d1

d2

d3

Fig d1–d3 *Stitching the flap at least 1cm (⅜in) above your pocket will allow for the bulk of the pocket so you can shut the flap neatly; view of the pocket with the flap raised – a magnetic snap fastening is used in this pocket; view of pocket with the flap down.*

Make it...
The Multi-Tasking Tote

This bag might be one of the most useful bags you'll ever make. It has pockets a-plenty – ten to be exact! The bag is also expandible with a wide flat base that opens up like a box, which makes one-handed search missions easy. This bag would be brilliant as a nappy bag or for picnics, shopping trips, crafting, college, overnight stays, or any occasion where you want to keep the contents of your bag organized and under control.

Side view *With all the fasteners closed, this roomy bag looks quite slim …*

Side view *… but undo the side poppers and the bag turns into a nice wide box that is super easy to see into and get into.*

Interior *The pockets are waiting to be stuffed with baby bottles, nappies and toys or could keep your craft, college, weekend trip, picnic, or beach gear organized.*

NEED TO KNOW

- You need plain coloured durable home dec fabrics for the exterior and the lining of this bag because all the pockets are unlined (to prevent too much bulk in the side seams).
- All seam allowances are 1cm (⅜in) unless stated.
- Pattern pieces are given in the pull-out section and include the 1cm (⅜in) seam allowance.

You will need

- 1 piece of plain coloured home dec fabric for exterior, 1m (1yd) x 1.5m (1½yd) wide
- 1 piece of plain coloured fabric for lining, 1m (1yd) x 1.5m (1½yd) wide
- 1 piece of home dec fabric for pocket trim, handles and ties, 50cm (½yd) x 1.5m (1½yd) wide
- Single-sided fusible fleece, 1m (1yd)
- Sewing threads to match the fabrics
- Magnetic snap closure, 18mm (¾in)
- 2 popper snaps, 1.5cm (½in)
- 4 eyelets, 11mm (½in)
- Fusible interfacing for eyelet and magnetic snap reinforcement, 20cm (8in)
- 6 metal bag feet (optional)
- Grid bag bottom and strong double-sided tape
- 4 cord stoppers and 4 cord ends (optional)
- Loop turner or large safety pin
- Disappearing marker
- Cotton or linen pressing cloth

Preparation

Cut the fabric and interfacing pieces as follows:

From The Multi-Tasking Tote (main body) pattern piece (see pull-out section)

- 2 x exterior fabric
- 2 x lining fabric
- 2 x fusible fleece

From The Multi-Tasking Tote (front/back pocket) pattern piece (see pull-out section)

- 2 x exterior fabric

From The Multi-Tasking Tote (lining pocket) pattern piece (see pull-out section)

- 2 x lining fabric

From The Multi-Tasking Tote (handle base) pattern piece (see pull-out section)

- 2 x exterior fabric

Then turn the pattern over and cut:

- 2 x exterior fabric (in mirror image)

From The Multi-Tasking Tote (handle) pattern piece (see pull-out section)

- 2 x exterior fabric
- 2 x lining fabric

Transfer all pattern notches and markings to the fabric with a disappearing marker

Also cut:

- 2 pieces of exterior fabric, 2 of lining fabric and 2 of fusible fleece, 32 x 20cm (12½ x 8in), for the bag sides
- 1 piece of exterior fabric, 1 of lining fabric and 1 of fusible fleece, 40 x 20cm (15¾ x 8in), for the bag base
- 2 pieces of exterior fabric, 29 x 20cm (11½ x 8in), for the exterior side pockets
- 2 pieces of trim fabric, 29 x 10cm (11½in x 4in), for the exterior side pocket trim
- 2 pieces of trim fabric, 40 x 14cm (15¾ x 5½in), for the exterior front/back pocket trim
- 2 pieces of trim fabric, 48 x 14cm (19 x 5½in), for the lining pocket trim
- 2 strips of trim fabric, 84 x 3cm (33 x 1⅛in), for the ties
- 2 pieces of fusible interfacing, 7 x 2.5cm (2¾ x 1in), for the eyelet reinforcement
- 2 pieces of lining fabric, 10cm (4in) square, for the magnetic snap tabs
- 2 pieces of fusible interfacing, 10 x 2.5cm (4 x 1in), for the magnetic snap reinforcement

> ### Label logic ...
> As there are quite a few pieces to this bag, it's worth labelling and interfacing (if necessary) each piece as you cut it to prevent confusion.

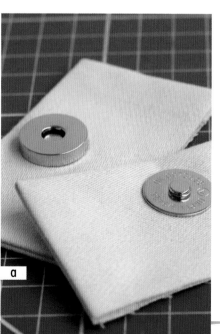

a

The tabs, handles, ties and bound edge pockets

1 **Make up the magnetic snap tabs** – take one of the magnetic snap tab fabric pieces, fold in half RST and iron the fold. Open up and place one of the magnetic snap fusible reinforcement pieces just above the fold on the WS and iron in place. Make an 'X' mark for the magnetic snap 1½cm (½in) up from the fold. Follow step 2 of magnetic snaps on page 91. Fold the magnetic snap in half RST and stitch along both side edges. Clip the corners, turn RSO, and iron. See **Fig a**. Repeat for the other magnetic snap fabric piece and snap half.

Fig a *These magnetic snap tabs will be sewn into the bag lining later.*

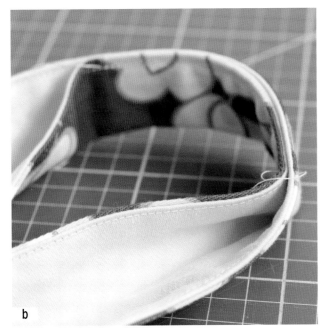

b

2 Make up the bag handles – bring one of the handle lining and handle exterior pieces RST and follow steps 2–4 of two-faced straps on page 104. Take the handle RSU and fold the centre of the handle in half RST. Stitch a 10cm (4in) line of stitches along the open edge along the centre only. See **Fig b**. Repeat for the other handle.

3 Make up the bag ties – take one of the tie fabric pieces RSU, fold in both long edges 5mm (³⁄₁₆in) and iron. Fold in half lengthways RST, iron and stitch along the open long edge. Divide into two equal lengths. Repeat with the other tie fabric piece.

4 Gather the top and bottom edges of front/back pockets – stitch gathering stitches along the top and bottom edges of the pocket 5mm (³⁄₁₆in) up from the edge. Gather the pocket fabric until it is the same width at the top and the bottom as the main body fabric piece. For sewing gathering stitches and gathering the fabric see step 3 on page 56. Repeat with the other front/back pocket piece.

5 Bind the top edges of all the pockets – the three different pockets are bound as follows:

• The side pockets: take one of the side pocket trim pieces WSU and fold in both long edges 1cm (³⁄₈in) and iron. Fold the trim (almost) in half lengthways so that the leading edge is 5mm (³⁄₁₆in) down from the other edge and iron the crease. See **Fig c**. Use this binding to bind the top edge of a side pocket, following steps 2 and 4 of bound edges on page 143. Repeat for the other side pocket and pocket trim.

• The lining pockets: bind the top edges of the lining pockets in the same way as the side pockets.

• The front/back pockets: make the front/back binding in the same way as for the other pockets. Open up the binding and on the shorter (height) side of the binding, interface the centre of the binding for the tie holes. Make two marks for eyelets 4cm (1½in) apart in the eyelet area. See **Fig d**. Insert the eyelets as per the instructions on the pack. Repeat with the other two eyelets and front/back binding. Thread the ties through each of the eyelet holes. Pin the opposite end of the ties to the binding to prevent them from escaping out of the eyelets. Thread on the cord stoppers and cord ends on to the ties (if using) and knot the ends of the ties. Bind the top edges of the pockets in the same way as the other pockets.

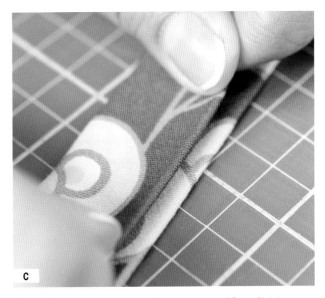

c

Fig c *Fold the binding nearly in half so there is gap of 5mm (³⁄₁₆in) between the two edges.*

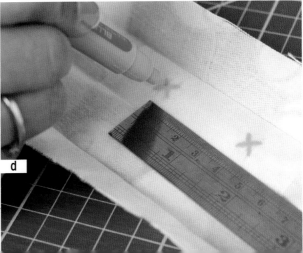

d

Fig d *Make markings for the eyelets on the shorter side of the binding – the shorter side will end up on the front of the pocket.*

The bag exterior

6 **Interface the exterior fabric pieces** – match the fusible interfacing pattern pieces to their partner exterior fabric pattern pieces and iron them to the WS of the fabric pieces.

7 **Make up the bellows side pockets** – take one of the trimmed side pocket fabric pieces RSU and measure and mark 7cm (2¾in) and 5cm (2in) in from both side edges. These are the concertina fold lines for the bellows. Make the bellow pockets following step 1 on page 126 (only fold the concertina at the marks you have just made).

8 **Stitch the bellows pockets to the exterior side panels** – place a bellows pocket RSU onto the bottom edge of one of the RS exterior side panels and match the side and bottom edges of the pocket and the exterior side panel. Pin and stitch the pocket to the exterior side panel at the bottom and side edges with a 5mm (³⁄₁₆in) seam allowance. Repeat for the other bellows pocket and side panel.

9 **Stitch the handle bases to the main body exterior** – take one of the handle base fabric pieces RSU, fold in the diagonal edge and short edge under 5mm (³⁄₁₆in) and iron. Place the handle base onto one of the RS top corner exterior main body pieces. Match up the raw top and side edges of the handle base and main body, pin and topstitch all around the handle base 3mm (⅛in) from the edge. See **Fig e**.

10 **Stitch the front/back pockets to the exterior main body pieces** – place a front/back pocket RSU onto the bottom edge of one of the RS exterior main body fabric pieces. Pin and stitch the pocket to the exterior main body at the sides and bottom with a 5mm (³⁄₁₆in) seam allowance. As you sew on the side top edges ensure you catch the tie ends in your stitches. See **Fig f**.

11 **Stitch the exterior side panels and main body pieces together** – bring one of the side panels and the main body pieces RST, pin and stitch together stopping 1cm (⅜in) up from the bottom edge – be sure to sew several securing stitches at both ends. Pin and stitch another side panel to the side edge of the main body in the same way. Continue until you have stitched together all four sides of the exterior bag.

12 **Stitch the exterior bag base to the exterior bag** – bring the short edges of the exterior bag and the base RST, pin and stitch together, stopping and starting 1cm (⅜in) from the edge (sewing securing stitches at both ends as in step 11). Repeat for the long edges of the base and bag. Clip off the corners and turn the bag RSO.

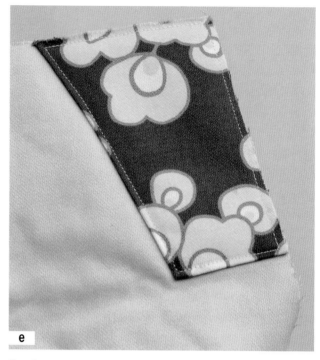

e

Fig e *Topstitch the handle base to the main body exterior fabric with a 3mm (⅛in) seam allowance.*

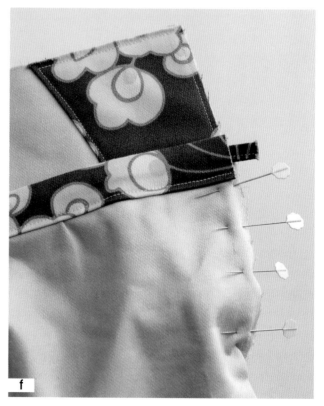

f

Fig f *Sew over the tie end as you sew the pocket to the body to secure it to the side seams.*

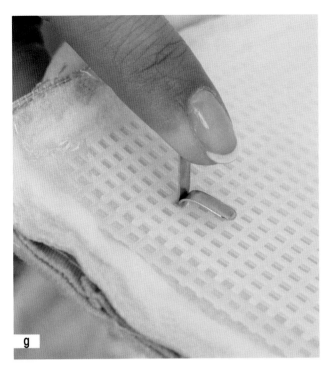

g

Fig g Push the prongs of the bag feet through the RS of the base and the grid bag bottom. This (along with the double-sided tape) will prevent the bag bottom from moving around in the bag.

13 **Insert the grid bag bottom and bag feet into the base** – (if using) if not using a bag bottom and bag feet proceed to step 14. Turn the bag upside down and measure the height and width of the base (from seam to seam) then subtract 5mm (³/₁₆in) from both measurements. Cut the grid bag bottom to this size and trim off the corner tips. Mark the position of the bag feet on the RS of the bag base. I like to place my bag feet 1.5cm (½in) in from the edge. Make corresponding marks for the bag feet on the grid bag bottom and make tiny scissor nicks in it to accommodate the feet prongs. Apply several strips of double-sided tape across the length of the grid bag bottom and press firmly in place into the bottom WS exterior bag. Take one of the bag feet and push the prongs through the RS of the bag base. Push the prongs right through the grid bag bottom and push down to secure. See **Fig g**. Repeat for the other bag feet.

14 **Stitch the handles to the bag exterior** – match the RS of the handle ends to the handle bases on the RS top edge of the exterior bag and pin in position. Lift up the handle to check that the handle is aligned with the diagonal edge of the handle base. The handle should appear to 'flow' into the handle base. See **Fig a** on page 75. Reposition the handle if necessary, match up the raw edges of the handle and the handle base and stitch with a 5mm (³/₁₆in) seam allowance. Repeat for the other bag handle.

The bag lining

15 **Stitch the magnetic snap tabs to the main body pieces** – take one of the magnetic snap tabs with the magnetic snap facing out and stitch it to the RS centre top edge one of the lining main body pieces with a 5mm (³/₁₆in) seam allowance. Repeat with the other magnetic snap tab and lining main body piece.

16 **Measure and mark the lining pocket divider lines** – take one of the lining pocket pieces and with the pocket RSU, measure and mark 15cm (6in) in from both side top edges with disappearing marker. Make corresponding marks directly below both marks on the bottom edge and mark the line between the two points. See step 11 on page 80.

17 **Stitch the pockets to the main body pieces** – place the pocket RSU onto the RS of the lining main body. Match up the pocket divider lines on the pocket to the pocket divider pattern markings on the main body pattern piece and pin and stitch in place.. Match up the pocket divider lines on the pocket and the lining and pin and stitch in place. Stitch the pocket to the main body along both pocket side edges with a 5mm (³/₁₆in) seam allowance. At the bottom edge of the divided pockets fold and pin small concertina pleat folds by the divider lines. As you fold the concertina at the side edges of the pocket piece ensure you leave enough clearance for the main body 1cm (³/₈in) seam allowance. See **Fig i**. Match up the raw bottom edges of the pocket and the lining body and stitch along the bottom edge with a 5mm (³/₁₆in) seam allowance. Repeat steps 16 and 17 for the other pocket and lining main body piece.

18 **Pin and stitch the lining bag together** – make up the lining bag in the same way as the exterior bag in steps 11 and 12 on page 136 except you need to leave a gap of 18cm (7in) in one of the side edges for turning out, and you do not need to turn the bag RSO.

i

Fig i Make small concertina folds at the bottom sides of the individual pockets. Leave enough space at the side pocket edges for sewing the lining together.

Assembling the bag

19 **Stitch the lining bag to the exterior bag** – insert the exterior bag RSO into the lining bag WSO. The right sides of the exterior bag and the lining bag should now be touching each other. Ensure the handles and the magnetic snap tabs are tucked down out of the way. Pin and stitch all around the top edge. See step 4 of pull through and turn out lining method on page 75.

20 **Turn the bag right side out** – reach into the gap in the lining and pull the exterior bag out through the hole. Push the exterior bag into the lining. Stitch the gap in the lining shut by pushing the raw edges of the gap in the lining into the hole and topstitching shut. Smooth out any bumps and iron the bag, paying extra attention to neatening the top edge. See steps 5 and 6 of pull through and turn out lining method on page 75.

21 **Topstitch the top of the bag** – fold both magnetic snap tabs down onto the lining and pin in place ready for stitching in the tabs in a down position. See **Fig j**. Topstitch all around the bag top edge with a 1cm (⅜in) seam allowance. Take your time as you sew over the magnetic snap tabs, as it will be a little bumpy.

22 **Apply popper snaps to the bag gusset** – on both sides of the gusset, measure and mark an 'X' 1.5cm (½in) down from the gusset top edge and 1.5cm (½in) in from the side seams for the popper snap placement. Follow the instructions on the packet to insert the popper snaps to the top edge of the bag gusset. See **Fig k**.

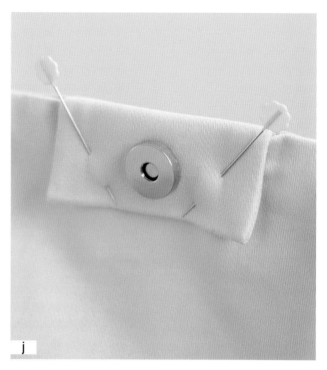

Fig j *Fold the magnetic snap tab down completely and pin in place.*

Fig k1–k2 *Insert the popper snaps into both gusset side top edges through all fabric layers.*

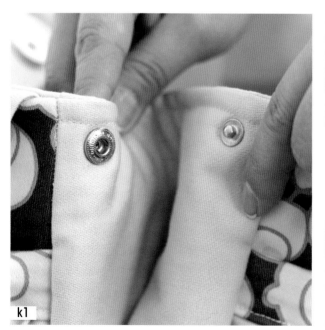

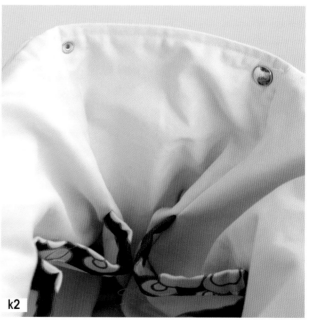

Right *The poppers are so handy – fill your bag then snap them shut to keep everything under control. Then when you need to get in there for a good look around, unpop and your ready to go!*

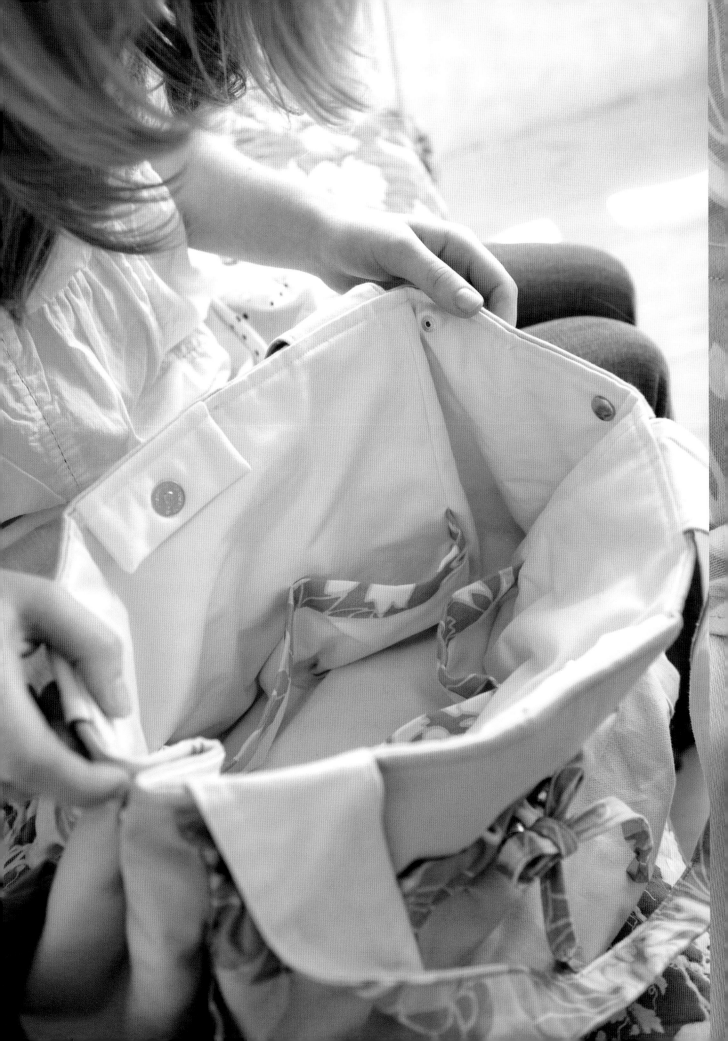

8: EDGINGS AND TRIMMINGS

The saying goes that it's the small things that make all the difference and sometimes that definitely rings true. In the same way that it's nice to adorn ourselves with pretty bracelets and necklaces we can also have fun adorning our bags. This chapter is all about edging and accessorizing your arm candy. The pages that follow look at two different ways of professionally trimming the edges of your bags, and after that we're going window-shopping for some ready-made bag trimmings.

Upcycle and away ...
This is the perfect opportunity to bring old ribbon, beads and baubles back to life.

EDGE/TRIM TYPE	APPLICATION AND BENEFITS	VARIETIES
Binding: page 142	Sewn along edges to cover raw edges. Use in matching or contrasting tones and use different textures for tactile interest. Reinforces edges.	Straight or bias. Shop-bought or homemade (see opposite).
Piping: page 144	Sewn between two layers so that the trim runs along the edge. Reinforces edges and defines shapes.	Thick or thin, matching or contrasting, twisted cord. Make your own piping for a huge choice of colours (see pages 144–145).
Ready-made Trim: page 146	Sewn along edges of bag or bag flaps. Adds eye-catching movement and gives an instant effect.	Beaded, pom-pom, feather boa, sequin fringe.
Ribbon: page 146	Very versatile sewn straight as binding, or decorative bands of colour, or used as embellishment (made into tassels, bows and corsages).	Silk, velvet, georgette, chiffon, wired, metallic, grosgrain, sequin, beaded, embroidered.
Jewellery: page 147	Pin corsages or brooches onto flaps or handles. Add lengths of beads to corsages or make you own bag charms. Make interchangeable wrist handles from colourful bangles. Items can be swapped to vary the look.	French beaded flowers, modern or antique brooches, hatpins, enamelled badges, beaded necklaces/bracelets, bangles.
Embellishments: page 147	Apply anywhere you want to zhush up your creations.	Tassels, buttons, beads, yo-yo, appliqué patches, sequins, fabric flowers, self-cover buttons.

Bound Edges You've probably seen how effective binding looks on quilts; well it also looks very cool on bags. Binding adds an attractive picture-frame effect. Try binding your pocket tops for starters. See pages 142–143.

Piped Edges Piping is an attractive and professional-looking way to trim seams. It is also an effective way to reinforce the seams, helping your bags to maintain their shape. The thicker the piping the more support it will provide. See pages 144–145.

Two types of binding – straight or bias

In order to bind or pipe your edges you need some fabric binding tape. You can use binding tape that is cut on the straight grain or tape that is cut on the bias. The choice of binding you use is determined by the shape of the edge that you want to bind. Curved edges need to be edged with binding that is cut on the bias. This is because bias-cut tape can be applied to curved edges without it wrinkling up. Shop-bought binding is usually pre-folded satin or cotton tape cut on the bias – which is why it's called bias binding. You can also make your own bias binding (see box). If you are only edging straight edges you can cut your own binding strips along the straight grain. If in doubt, stick to bias binding, which is perfect for both curved and straight edges. All the techniques and the project in this chapter will make use of bias binding.

MAKING YOUR OWN BIAS BINDING

It might be faster to buy bias binding, but you will be limited to the colours and the widths available in the shop. Why not try making your own pretty bias binding in fabrics of your choice?

One thing you'll need is a bias tape maker to speed things up. Available in different widths, a bias tape maker creates the two binding folds ready for you to iron them in place. Cut the fabric strips to the height stated on the instructions of your bias tape maker. To cut the strip on the bias, cut the fabric at 45 degrees from the selvage. To make a long continuous strip of binding trim the ends of the strips at 45 degrees. Overlap the two fabric ends RST, pin and stitch with a 1cm (⅜in) seam allowance. Trim off both of the small triangles of fabric that stick out from the sides. Iron the seam open and pass through the bias tape maker as per the instructions on the pack. See **Fig a**.

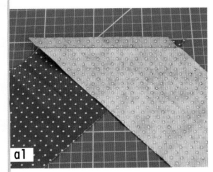
a1

a2

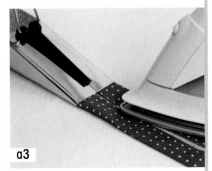
a3

Fig a1–a3 *Join the 45-degree ends of the strap RST as shown and stitch together; trim off the small protruding triangles; pass the joined tape through tape maker and iron the folds.*

Bound Edges

Binding an edge has the effect of adding an attractive fabric border to the edge. This makes it a good way of adding a flash of colour and strengthening the edge. Try binding the top edges of pockets, the top edge of your bag or your bag flaps.

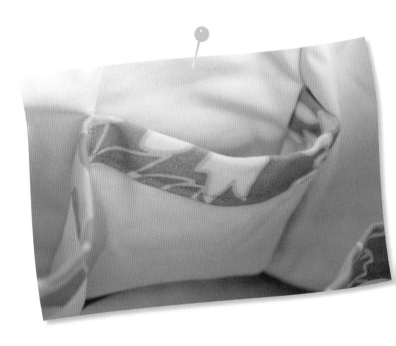

You will need

- 1 strip of folded and pressed shop-bought or homemade bias binding (see page 141). To gauge the height and length of your binding see Need To Know

NEED TO KNOW

- To gauge the height of the binding tape, decide on the height of the finished bound edge, multiply that by 4 and add 3mm (⅛in). If you want your finished bound edges to be 1cm (⅜in) tall, your binding will need to be 4.3cm (1⅝in).
- To gauge the length of the binding, measure around all around the edge of the item and add 8cm (3⅛in) for folding in.
- All seam allowances are 5mm (³⁄₁₆in) unless stated otherwise.
- If trimming pocket tops, make up your pocket and add the binding BEFORE stitching the pocket to your bag. Fold in both short edges of the binding at either end so as to conceal the raw edges.
- If trimming bag flaps, make up your flap and apply the binding BEFORE stitching the flap to your bag.

a

1 **Fold and press the binding** – take the pre-folded binding tape and press an off-centre crease across the length of the binding. See **Fig a**.

Fig a *Fold the binding lengthways so that the bottom folded edge doesn't quite meet the top folded edge.*

2 **Stitch the open binding to the edge** – with the shorter folded side facing upwards unfold the binding. With binding opened and WSU, fold in the short edge at the start of the binding. Place the top edge of the opened binding WSU onto the RS top edge. Ensure that you are pinning the shorter folded side (from step 1) to the item. Match the edges and pin all around. When you almost reach the end of the item, trim the excess binding so that the ends overlap. Pin in place. Stitch the binding to the top edge of the item with a 3mm (⅛in) seam allowance. See **Fig b**.

3 **Alternatively, stitch the open binding to the pocket top edge** – if you are binding a pocket top, fold in the short edge first before your begin pinning. When you reach the end of the pocket fold in the short edge again as before. Stitch the binding to the top edge of the item with a 3mm (⅛in) seam allowance.

4 **Fold up the binding and topstitch to finish** – fold the binding back up over the top edge of the item. The folded off-centre crease of the binding (from step 1) should butt up snugly with the top edge of the item. Pin the folded binding in position. You'll notice that the binding is taller on the WS. Stitch the binding close to the bottom edge of the binding on the RS of the item. The stitches from the front will easily catch the bottom edge of the binding on the WS because the WS binding is taller. See **Fig c**.

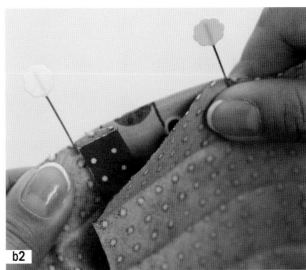

Fig b1–b2 *Fold in the edge at the start of the binding before pinning. The end of the binding is trimmed long enough to overlap the start of the binding thus concealing the raw edge.*

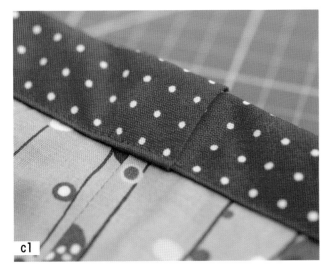

Fig c1–c2 *The result from the front and from the back. Because the binding is taller at the back, the stitches from the front will easily catch the bottom edge of the binding at the back.*

Piped Edges

A fine strip of coloured piping adds impact. Pipe the top, bottom and side edges and/or flaps of your bags. This tutorial shows how to make piping and how to insert a continuous line of piping around the top edge of a bag. To see how to pipe the side and bottom edge of your bags see steps 6–9 on pages 151–152.

You will need

- 1 strip of bias-cut fabric to cover the cord. To gauge the height and length of your binding see Need To Know
- 1 length of piping cord the same length of the bias-cut strip
- Piping sewing machine foot
- Seam ripper
- Disappearing marker

NEED TO KNOW

⊕ This top edge piping technique needs to be used in conjunction with the pull through and turn out method of inserting bag linings. See pages 74–75.

⊕ To gauge the height of the piping covering, measure your piping cord around the perimeter, and add two lots of your seam allowance, plus 3mm (⅛in).

⊕ To gauge the length of the piping, measure around all around the edge of the item and add 5cm (2in) for folding in.

⊕ All seam allowances are 5mm (³⁄₁₆in) unless stated otherwise.

⊕ When piping the top edge of your bag, apply the piping to the RS of the exterior bag AFTER you have finished constructing the exterior and BEFORE you sew the lining to the exterior.

In the groove ...

A piping foot really speeds up piping making and sewing. It has a groove running vertically on the underside, which keeps the piping cord under control while you stitch it into the fabric covering.

a

Fig a *The start of the piping is fully stitched in while the other end is left open by 5cm (2in) for folding in.*

1 **Make up the piping** – to cut bias fabric strips for covering the piping see page 141, disregarding the information about the bias tape maker. Fold the bias strip in half WST, iron, open out, and lay the cord down the centre crease. The cord needs to butt right up against the crease. Attach the piping foot to your sewing machine and position the cord underneath the groove in the foot. Adjust the needle position 3mm (⅛in) to the right of the edge of the cord and stitch the piping stopping 5cm (2in) from the end. See **Fig a**.

2 Begin to stitch the piping to the bag exterior – lay the raw top edge of the piping onto the RS top edge of the bag exterior back (this way the piping join won't be on display at the front of your bag.) Match up the raw edges and pin. With the piping foot still attached to your machine begin stitching the piping 4cm (1½in) in from the end. Ensure that your stitches lie slightly to the right of the piping stitches made in step 1. Stitch all around the bag top edge 5cm (2in) short of the end of the piping. See **Fig b**.

Fig b *The open-ended part of the piping is on the left side. This gap between the piping ends will make it easier for you to create a join in the piping in the next step.*

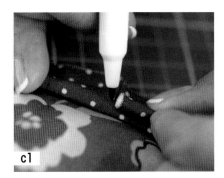 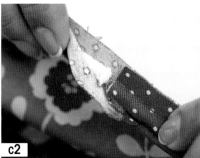 

Fig c1 *Make a mark where the start of the piping (on the right) falls onto the end of the piping (on the left).* **Fig c2** *Unpick a few stitches in the piping and trim the piping to the mark you made previously. Fold in the short edge of the open end of the piping (on the left) then lay the closed end of the piping (on the right) inside the open end. The piping cord ends should now be touching each other.* **Fig c3** *The result will be a neat join on the piping.*

3 Create a join in the piping – lay the open-ended part of the piping flat against the bag top edge, and then lay the sealed part of the piping on top of the open end as shown. Make a mark where the sealed end of the piping falls onto the open end. See **Fig c1**. Now trim the piping cord inside the open end of your piping to the mark that you just made. If necessary use a seam ripper to undo any stitches to allow you access to the piping cord. Fold in the short edge of the open end of the piping and lay the closed end of the piping into the open end. See **Fig c2**. Fold up the ends of the open-ended piping (with the sealed end tucked inside), pin and stitch the piping ends starting and stopping at your original stitches (from step 2). See **Fig c3**.

4 Stitch the lining and the exterior together (with piping sandwiched in between) – make up the bag lining (leaving a gap in the bottom edge of the lining for turning out) (see step 1 on page 74). Insert the bag exterior RSO into the bag lining WSO. The RS of the two bags should now be touching each other. Match the raw top edges and side seams and pin. Firmly run your fingernail along the piping edge (through the lining) so you can more clearly see the outline of the piping underneath. With the piping foot still attached to your machine position the piping underneath the groove of the piping foot. Stitch as close as you can to the piping without actually stitching though it. See **Fig d**. Stitch all around the top edge of the bag. The piping is now attached and you can continue with the rest of the bag construction (see page 156).

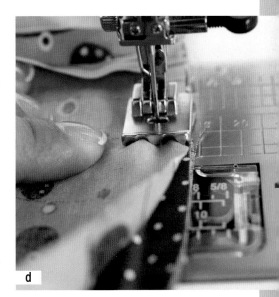

Fig d *Position the needle as close as you can to the piping without sewing through the piping.*

Shopping for Trimmings

When it comes to trimming and embellishing a bag I admit that I am a quick-fix ready-made kind of girl. Appliqué and embroidery can look gorgeous on bag and purses, but these techniques are not really my forte. However, there are plenty of good books and websites that can educate you on the finer points of these slower crafts. Ready-made doesn't mean that I always go shopping for my trimmings, though. Here are some trimmings and suggestions for their use on bags:

At source ...
Sometimes the most interesting embellishments come from surprising sources (see pages 35 and 107).

Pom-pom and beaded trim I don't know any sewist that doesn't like colourful fluffy pom-pom trim. Try adding pom-pom trim to the bottom edges of your bags or bag flaps. Beaded trim when used on evening bags adds an expensive-looking finishing touch. I have gone to town with dangly trim on this bag. I have layered pom-pom trim on top of some pretty beaded trim.

Ribbon Trimming your bags with ribbon is quick and effective. Try prettying up a plain coloured bag with an oversized patterned ribbon bow or stitching a piece of embroidered ribbon across the width of a plain linen bag. Adding a satin/velvet bow on a same-coloured purse always looks fabulous. I've collected pretty ribbon from relatives, holidays and a bit of stash swapping with craft friends. I have (handbag) plans for all of them of course.

Tassels There are some gorgeous fabric and/or beaded tassels available in the shops. Look in the curtain-making section of fabric stores or look for key tassels. Or even make your own. I love to add tassels to the bottom edge of flaps or to handle loops for a bit of instant colour, movement and boho chic!

Vintage brooches Sometimes I love nothing more than poking around in charity shops or flea markets for old costume jewellery. I think the older vintage costume jewellery has a lot of charm and humour. Brooches are an instant way to add that charm to your bags and best of all you can change the brooch to suit your mood … and your outfit.

Flower corsages It may be a classic combination, but a big silk flower on an evening bag is always going to look gorgeous. There's no need to stop at evening purses and silk flowers. Fabric flowers look great on all sorts of bags. Ready-made fabric flowers are easily available from shops and you can also easily and quickly make your own flowers using fabric yo-yo makers (see page 43).

Self-cover buttons Few things are cuter than a bunch of cheerful coordinating self-cover buttons that you have whipped up yourself. Choose a nice fabric print and the self-cover buttons will look sweet enough to wear as badges – but they'll look even nicer placed onto your bags and purses. Use them for button and loop closures (see page 42), grouped in a pretty formation, or even as the centre of a fabric flower. They are quick to make (just follow the instructions on the packet) and are a brilliant way to use up fabric scraps.

Make it...
The Piping-Hot Hobo

Although this bag looks technically advanced, it is not as tricky as you might think. The secret lies in its round shape – the curved edges make the piping a breeze. The piping and tassel trim on this bag, though simple, both make a strong graphic statement. But what you'll love most is the wide collapsible gusset, which makes the bag slim when less full and curvy-licious when it's brimming with gear.

Side view *With the side poppers closed the bag has a slim line and clean profile. The piping really defines the edges and gives the bag a very professional touch.*

Gusset *The side poppers open to reveal a wider gusset and a roomier bag.*

Interior *The curved top edge at the front is a nice design detail that echoes the round shape of the bag and it makes for easier access to your bag essentials. Inside is a simple slip pocket.*

NEED TO KNOW

☙ Heavier weight fabrics for the exterior are not recommended; medium-weight fabric is best because during construction you will need to feel the piping cord underneath the exterior layer of fabric.

☙ Make the piping from a 2.5m x 3cm (2¾yd x 1⅛in) bias-cut fabric strip and 2.5m x 5–6mm (2¾yd x ¼in) piping cord. See pages 144–145.

☙ If you do not want to make one continuous length of piping cord, you will need two 78cm (30¾in), one 30cm (12in) and one 64cm (25in) lengths of piping cord for this project.

☙ All seam allowances are 1cm (⅜in) unless stated otherwise.

☙ Pattern pieces are given in the pull-out section and include the 1cm (⅜in) seam allowance.

You will need

- 1 piece of medium-weight fabric for exterior, 50cm (½yd) x 112cm (44in) wide
- 1 piece of quilt- to medium-weight cotton fabric for lining, 50cm (½yd) x 112cm (44in) wide
- Medium-weight woven fusible interfacing, 50cm (½yd)
- Fusible fleece, 50cm (½yd)
- Piping cord to compliment the exterior fabric, 2.5m (2¾yd)
- Strip of bias fabric the same colour as the piping for the flap trim band, 45 x 3cm (17¾ x 1⅛in)
- Sewing threads to match the fabrics
- Ready-made bag strap with trigger hooks/bolt snaps, approx 125 x 1.5cm (49¼ x ½in)
- Magnetic snap closure, 18mm (¾in)
- 2 D-rings as wide as your bag strap
- 2 popper snaps, 1.5cm (½in)
- Tassel to match the colour of your piping and trim, 2.5cm (1in) wide
- Piping sewing machine foot (optional but very helpful – see page 145)
- Seam ripper
- Hera marker (optional)
- Loop turner or safety pin
- Disappearing marker

Preparation

Cut the fabric and interfacing pieces as follows:

From The Piping-Hot Hobo (body front) pattern piece (see pull-out section)

- 1 x exterior fabric
- 1 x fusible fleece
- 1 x fusible interfacing
- 1 x lining fabric

From The Piping-Hot Hobo (body back) pattern piece (see pull-out section)

- 1 x exterior fabric
- 1 x fusible fleece
- 1 x fusible interfacing
- 1 x lining fabric

From The Piping-Hot Hobo (gusset) pattern piece (see pull-out section)

- 1 x exterior fabric
- 1 x fusible fleece
- 1 x fusible interfacing
- 1 x lining fabric

From The Piping-Hot Hobo (flap) pattern piece (see pull-out section)

- 1 x exterior fabric
- 1 x fusible fleece
- 1 x fusible interfacing
- 1 x lining fabric

Transfer all pattern notches and markings to the fabric with a disappearing marker

Also cut:

- 2 pieces of lining fabric, 25 x 16cm (10 x 6¼in), for the inner lined slip pocket
- 1 piece of exterior fabric, 14 x 5cm (5½ x 2in), for the handle loops
- 2 pieces of fusible interfacing, 2.5cm (1in) square, for the magnetic snap reinforcement

Interfacing and central gusset seam

1 Interface the exterior fabric pieces – match the fusible interfacing pattern pieces to their partner exterior fabric pieces and iron them to the WS of the fabric pieces. Iron the magnetic snap reinforcement interfacing squares to the WS of the bag exterior front and the bag lining flap pieces, behind the markings for the magnetic snap. Finally, iron the fusible fleece pattern pieces onto the WS of all of the exterior fabric pieces (directly onto the fusible interfacing).

2 Stitch a central seam into the gusset fabric pieces – take the exterior gusset piece and fold it in half lengthways RST. Pin the fold in place and stitch along the folded edge with a 3mm (⅛in) seam allowance. See **Fig a**. Repeat with the gusset lining piece, except fold it WST.

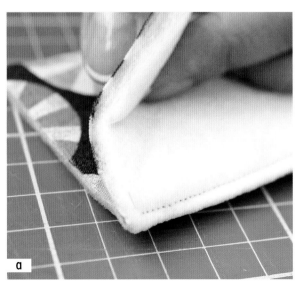

a

Fig a *This simple but clever centre seam will make the bag gusset easily and neatly collapsible..*

The handle loops

3 **Make up the handle loops** – take the handle loop fabric piece and follow the steps on page 102 to make one open-end strap. Divide the resulting strap into two equal lengths and thread a D-ring onto each of the handle loops.

4 **Pin and stitch the handle loops to the exterior back fabric piece** – take one of the handle loops (folded in half with D-ring still attached) and place it onto one of the handle loop pattern markings on the RS bag exterior fabric piece. Match up the raw edges. Hold the handle loop in place with your fingers and stitch to the RS bag exterior with a 5mm (³⁄₁₆in) seam allowance. Repeat with the other handle loop. See **Fig b**.

The bag exterior

5 **Insert the magnetic snap to the exterior front** – follow the steps on page 91 to insert the magnetic part of the snap to the RS of the exterior bag front at the magnetic snap marking.

6 **Pin and stitch piping cord onto the exterior sides and bottom** – cut a 78cm (30¾in) length from the piping cord. Take the exterior front fabric and pin and stitch the piping cord to the RS sides and bottom. Starting and stopping at the pattern side edge piping markings, pin the piping to the RS of the bag front exterior. Ensure there is an equal length of excess piping at either end (which will be trimmed off later). Attach the piping foot to your sewing machine and use the same coloured thread as the piping to stitch the piping to the bag exterior fabric piece. The bottom edge pattern notches will now be concealed underneath the piping. Make small scissor nicks in the piping seam allowance to uncover the notch markings. See **Fig c**. Repeat with the bag exterior back and another 78cm (30¾in) length of piping cord.

Match it up ...
Take care to match the raw edges of the piping and the bag front exterior fabric neatly to give a slick, professional result.

b

Fig b *Stitch the handle loop to the exterior bag so the D-ring is pointing away from the edge of the fabric.*

c1

c2

Fig c1–c2 *Stitch the piping to the bag exterior. Stitch 3mm (⅛in) to the right of the piping itself; look for the notch markings underneath the piping cord and make small scissor nicks in the piping seam allowance (at the notch markings).*

7 Pin and stitch piping cord onto the bag front curved top edge – cut a 30cm (12in) length from the piping cord. Pin and stitch the piping cord to the RS bag front curved top edge as in step 6 on page 151.

8 Pin the gusset to the bag exterior – take the piping cord ends and bend them at right angles, pointing out of the bag fabric. See **Fig d**. Pin the RS of the exterior gusset to the RS of the bag exterior front (over the sticking-out piping cord ends). Take care to match the notch markings on both fabric pieces. Ensure there is an equal length of excess gusset fabric at either end (which will be trimmed off later). Pin on the gusset side.

9 Stitch the gusset to the bag exterior – use a Hera marker or your fingernail to trace firmly around the outline of the piping cord (through the gusset fabric) so you can more easily see it to sew around it. With the piping foot still attached, stitch the gusset to the bag exterior all around the sides and bottom. As you sew over the bumpy piping cord ends take care to help the piping foot engage (and disengage at the end) with the piping cord (feel for it through the gusset fabric). Stitch on the gusset side. Trim the excess piping off both sides close to the seams. Clip the curved seams. See **Fig e**. Repeat steps 8 and 9 to pin and stitch the gusset to the exterior back. Trim off the excess gusset fabric at both gusset top edges.

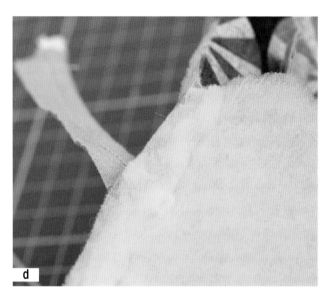

d

Fig d *Bend the piping cords down at 90 degrees so they stick out from the side edges.*

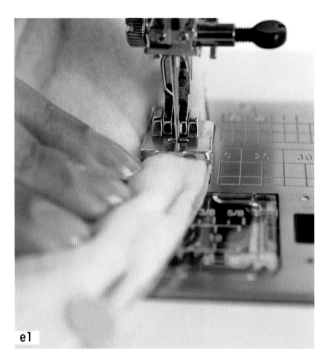

e1

Fig e1 - e2 *As you stitch the gusset to the exterior feel for the piping underneath the fabric. Stitch as close as you can to the piping without actually sewing through it; clip the curved seam to make the turned-out bag seams smooth.*

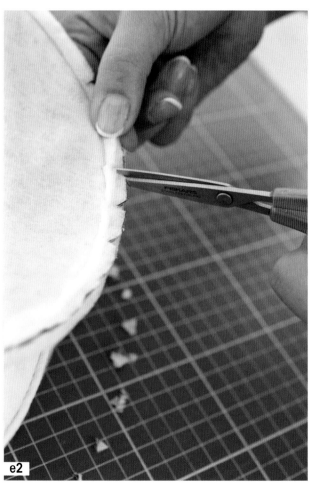

e2

The bag lining

10 **Insert a slip pocket into the lining** – take the lined slip pocket fabric pieces and follow the steps on page 125 to make a lined slip pocket. Pin and stitch the pocket to the RS centre of the lining back fabric 4cm (1½in) down from the top edge.

11 **Pin and stitch the lining bag together** – omitting the piping cord, assemble the lining as in steps 8 and 9 but leave a gap of 15cm (6in) in one of the bottom edges of the lining for turning out.

The bag flap

12 **Make the flap trim band and stitch onto the exterior flap** – divide the flap trim bias strip into two equal lengths. Bring the strips RST, pin and stitch together along both long edges with a 5mm (³⁄₁₆in) seam allowance. Iron the seams open and use a loop turner or safety pin to turn the tube RSO. Iron the band trim. Pin the band vertically to the centre RS of the bag flap exterior and topstitch in place along both long edges, close to the edge. See **Fig f**.

13 **Insert the magnetic snap to the flap lining** – follow the steps on page 91 to insert the non-magnetic part of the snap to the RS of the flap lining at the magnetic snap marking.

14 **Stitch the tassel to the flap lining** – place the head of the tassel onto the RS centre bottom edge of the lining (so the fringes of the tassel point towards the top edge of the flap lining). Stitch the tassel in place on the tassel loop cord with a 1cm (³⁄₈in) seam allowance. Stitch in forward and reverse a few times for extra strength. See **Fig g**. Trim off the excess cord loop from the tassel.

15 **Pin and stitch piping cord onto the flap exterior** – take the remaining length of piping cord and pin and stitch the cord to the exterior flap RS as in step 6 on page 151.

16 **Pin and stitch the flap lining to the flap exterior** – take the piping cord ends and bend them at right angles as in step 8. Pin the RS of the flap lining to the RS of the flap exterior (over the piping cord ends). Stitch the flap exterior and lining together as in step 9. Turn the flap RS, smooth out and using a pressing cloth, iron all over the RS and WS of the flap.

f

Fig f *Topstitch the band down the centre RS of the flap.*

Best foot forward ...
Though a piping foot is best for this project, you can also use a zipper foot to help you stitch close to the piping.

g

Fig g *Stitch over the loop cord of the tassel a few times for strength.*

Assembling the bag

17 Stitch the bag flap to the bag exterior – pin the bag flap WSU to the RS of the bag exterior. Place the bag flap onto the centre top edge of the bag exterior back. Match up the raw edges and stitch the flap to the exterior bag back with a 5mm (³⁄₁₆in) seam allowance. See step 19 on page 81.

18 Stitch the lining bag to the exterior bag – bend the piping cord ends on the curved top edge at right angles so they are sticking up from the top edge. Insert the exterior bag RSO into the lining bag WSO. The right sides of the exterior bag and the lining bag should now be touching each other. Pin all around the curved front top edge. Stitch all around the top edge, but stop to attach the piping foot to the sewing machine in order to sew around the curved hand piped top edge. See **Fig h**.

Fig h *The bag lining and the bag exterior have been pinned and stitched together. Now just snip off the excess piping ends.*

19 Turn the bag RSO – reach into the gap in the lining and pull the exterior bag out through the hole. Push the exterior bag into the lining. Push the raw edges of the lining into the hole and topstitch the gap shut. Smooth out any bumps and iron the bag (paying extra attention to neatening the top edge). See steps 5 and 6 of pull through and turn out lining method on page 75.

20 Topstitch the top of the bag – with the flap open topstitch all around the bag top edge with a 5mm (³⁄₁₆in) seam allowance. See **Fig i**.

21 Apply popper snaps to the bag gusset – on both sides of the gusset, measure and mark an 'X' 1.5cm (½in) down from the gusset top edge and 1.5cm (½in) in from the side seams for the popper snap placement. Follow the instructions on the packet to insert the popper snaps to the top edge of the bag gusset. See step 22 on page 139.

22 Finishing touches – clip the bag strap onto the D-rings of the handle loops and admire your work!

Confidence booster ...
If you don't feel confident about sewing the piping underneath the layers, try running a soft pencil along the edge of the piping (through the fabric layers). This will leave you with a clear guide to stitch along.

Fig i *As you topstitch around the top edge of the bag do not stitch onto the piping at the curved top edge at the front the bag. Keep to the 5mm (³⁄₁₆in) seam allowance from the top edge of the exterior fabric only.*

Right *This style of bag makes a great alternative to the traditional work handbag. The structure keeps it looking smart, while your choice of fabric and trim add unique personal style.*

Construction

One thing I love about bag making is after you have made a few bags you soon notice that some of the bag construction techniques and the order of construction are often similar from one bag to another. Far from being restricting, this repetition makes it easier to become more expert at bag making, thus leaving you with more brain space to design gorgeous bags. Effective bag design relies heavily on being able to plan the construction of a bag in your head. This knowledge comes with practice, but I'm going speed things up by listing the order of bag construction for you.

If you're a bag-making newbie, don't worry if this doesn't make that much sense now. After you've made two or three bags from this book, or any other patterns, you'll see that the list below describes how to make a given bag in general. It shows you what bag-making bits need to be done (and when they should be done) during the bag-making process. It should help jog your memory when you want to go on and design your own bags – and I bet it won't be long before that happens!

General order of bag making preparation

1 Make up handle loops (if using). See page 102.

2 Make up handles/straps (if using). See pages 100–109.

3 Make up bag flap (if using). Insert any closure into flap (if using) during flap construction. See pages 82–93.

4 Make up lining and/or exterior pockets (if using). See pages 64–71 and 122–131.

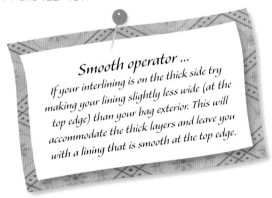

Smooth operator ...
If your interlining is on the thick side try making your lining slightly less wide (at the top edge) than your bag exterior. This will accommodate the thick layers and leave you with a lining that is smooth at the top edge.

General order of bag lining construction

1 Cut lining fabric pieces from the pattern.

2 Interface/interline fabric pieces (if using). See pages 31 and 36–39.

3 Insert pockets (if using) to lining fabric piece(s). See pages 66–71.

4 Insert darts/pleats/gusset/gathers/pleats (if using) to fabric lining pieces. See pages 46–56.

5 Add top edge fasteners such as magnetic snaps (if using) to lining pieces. See page 91.

6 Insert a concealed top-edge zip (if using). See pages 88–89.

7 Pin and stitch lining fabric pieces together (as detailed in each project).

8 Insert a flat bottom (if using). See pages 54, 120 and 137.

General order of bag exterior construction

1 Cut exterior fabric pieces.

2 Interface/interline fabric pieces (if using). See pages 31 and 36–39.

3 Insert pockets (if using) to exterior fabric piece(s).

4 Insert darts/pleats/gusset/gathers/pleats (if using) to fabric exterior pieces. See pages 48–56.

5 Add top edge fasteners such as twist locks/magnetic snaps etc. (if using) to exterior pieces. See pages 84–93.

6 Pin and stitch exterior fabric pieces together (as detailed in each project).

7 Insert flat bottom or grid bag bottom to exterior (if using). See pages 54, 120 and 137.

8 Insert bag feet (if using) to RS of bag exterior bottom. See page 137.

9 Stitch bag flap (if using) to RS of the bag exterior. See pages 62, 153, and 154.

10 *With ready-made bag handles attached (if using), stitch bag handle loops to the RS top edge of the bag exterior. See pages 110–111.

11 *Attach handmade bag straps (if using) to bag exterior top edge. See pages 102–109.

* The construction order of these steps vary depending on which lining insertion method you are using. See pages 72–75.

Suppliers

With the aid of a few mouse few clicks, your trusty credit card and your post box, a wealth of lovely bag making and craft supplies from all over the world can be yours. Any day is Christmas Day when a crafty package is delivered to your door! Here is a selection of my favourite online shops.

UK

U-Handbag
www.u-handbag.com
My one-stop shop for bag and purse making supplies, patterns and kits. We deliver worldwide.

Calico Laine
0151 336 3939
www.calicolaine.co.uk
For fabrics, trimmings and haberdashery

Cloth House
020 72871555
www.clothhouse.com
For beautiful trims, a wide range of fabrics and great quality faux leather

Clover
0081 (06) 6978-2220
www.clover-mfg.com/euro/index/english.html
For a huge range of haberdashery, quilting supplies and equipment

The Cotton Patch
0121 702 2840
www.cottonpatch.co.uk
For patchwork and quilting fabrics, books, wadding, notions and haberdashery

Fabric Rehab
www.fabricrehab.co.uk
For a good selection of quilt fabrics

Gutermann
020 85891642
www.gutermann.com
For fantastic quality sewing threads

Harris Tweed & Knitwear
01859 502040
www.harristweedandknitwear.co.uk
For Harris Tweed cloth by the metre – the genuine article and gorgeous!

Janome
0161 666 6011
www.janome.co.uk
My first purchased sewing machine was a Janome; 14 years on and I still sew with a Janome

John Lewis
0845 604 9049
www.johnlewis.com
For a good choice of decorator weight fabrics

Josy Rose
0845 450 1212
www.josyrose.com
For a wide selection of trimmings

Le Prevo
0191 232 4179
www.leprevo.co.uk
For leather, suede and craft supplies

MacCulloch & Wallis
020 7629 0311
www.macculloch-wallis.co.uk
For haberdashery and trimmings, including bridal

Millcroft Textiles
0115 926 3154
www.millcrofttextiles.co.uk
For a wide range of haberdashery and bridal and occasion fabrics

Norfolk Textiles
01263 768237
http://shop.norfolktextiles.co.uk
For a great choice of decorator weight fabrics including oilcloth

Prym
+49 (0)24 02/14 04
www.prym-consumer.com
For a huge range of haberdashery, equipment and trimmings

VV Rouleaux
020 7730 3125
www.vvrouleaux.com
For a wide selection of beautiful ribbons and trims

USA

Amy Butler
740-587-2841
www.amybutlerdesign.com
One of my favourite fabric designers (with a very inspirational website)

Clotilde
800-545-4002
www.clotilde.com
For sewing and quilting supplies. Lots of sewing advice on their website too

Create For Less
1-866-333-4463
www.createforless.com
For a huge sewing and craft supplies at discount prices

Dreamweaver Yarns
1-888-321 5648
www.dreamweaveryarns.com
For yarns and bag-making handles and hardware

Jo-Ann Fabric & Craft Stores
1-888-739-4120
www.joann.com
For sewing supplies in a one-stop shop

M & J Trimming
800-965-8746
www.mjtrim.com
For a wide choice of trimmings and accessories

Mood Fabrics
www.moodfabrics.com
For designer fabrics (when you want to push the boat out)

Purl Patchwork
800-597-7875
www.purlsoho.com
For fabric, yarns, and haberdashery – great blog too!

Sew Mama Sew
1-503-380-3584
www.sewmamasew.com
For a huge choice of modern quilting fabrics – and another great blog

Westminster Fibres
1-866-907-3305
www.westminsterfibers.com/fabric.html
Manufacturers of some of my favourite quilting fabrics including Amy Butler and Free Spirit

About the Author

Lisa Lam is a London College of Fashion graduate who owns U-Handbag.com – an online store specializing in bag-making supplies. At work (if you could call it that) she designs bags and regularly writes for craft magazines. She lives in Brighton with her husband Alan and their very friendly dog, Beans. Lisa's second home is the crafting community on the Internet (or crafti-verse) from which she blogs and where she is constantly amazed by the wealth of talent of her fellow crafters.

Visit her blog here:
www.u-handbag.typepad.com

Visit her shop here:
www.u-handbag.com

Acknowledgments

Big thanks to my customers and blog readers – your warmth and willingness to share is truly inspiring. Without you I would have to get a 'real' job. Thanks to Amy Butler for being a lovely lady, a craft hero and fabulous to work with. Thanks also go to the folks at David & Charles: Charly Bailey for her design talents, James Brooks for keeping calm, Jenny Fox-Proverbs for saying 'how about it?' and being my crafty confidante, and my amazing editor Ame Verso, inventor of the fine tooth comb. Thanks to my agent Jane Graham Maw for taking on 'unknown' me. Thanks to Chrissie Day for getting me into book writing. Lastly, thanks to Lorna and Jack at Bangwallop for taking the lush 'coffee table' worthy photos and for caring as much as I do about getting the perfect shot.

Index